CONTEMPORARY ISSUES IN MANAGEMENT

CONTEMPORARY ISSUES IN MANAGEMENT

By

Dr. Basant Mehta
Professor & Head
Deptt. of Banking & Financial Management
JRN Rajasthan Vidyapeeth University
Udaipur

DPH

DISCOVERY PUBLISHING HOUSE PVT. LTD.
NEW DELHI-110 002

Published by:
Tilak Wasan
DISCOVERY PUBLISHING HOUSE PVT. LTD.
4831/24, Ansari Road, Prahlad Street
Darya Ganj, New Delhi-110002 (India)
Phone: +91-11-23279245, 43764432
Fax: +91-11-23253475
E-mail: parul.wasan@gmail.com
info@discoverypublishinggroup.com
web: www.discoverypublishinggroup.com

***First Edition:* 2011**
ISBN: 978-81-8356-714-5

Contemporary Issues in Management

Preface

Management is a problem solving process of effectively achieving objectives through the efficient use of scarce resources in a changing environment with changing business practices and increasing social responsibility of organizations, the role of Managers has become all the significant. Management is essential to any kind of organizations. Wherever there are group of people working together to achieve some common objectives, it becomes essential to guide, organize and control them. The tern 'Management' applies to any organization irrespective of the size or nature of operations. The prime concern of a 'Manager' is to manage their people and resources effectively. In one context, it may comprise the activities of executives and administrative personnel in an organization. While in another, it may refer to a system of getting things done. In a broad perspective, Management can be considered as the proper utilization of people and other resources in an organization to accomplish desired objectives.

This book has been endowed with views of Scholars and Professors on different facets of Management. An assortment of articles and research papers has been included in this book to offer a wide range of knowledge on the matter of concern. This book is an attempt to review and present the current state of knowledge of Marketing Management, Human Recourse Management, Financial Management and Information Technology. This book is provide a means of comprehensive study of the various issues of management in a simple, lucid and easy way.

This book is a compilation of research articles contributed by Management Scholars. I am thankful to paper contributors of this book.

I am also grateful to Mr. Wason of Discovery Publishing House for taking keen interest in timely publication of this book.

Prof. Basant Mehta

List of Contributors

1. *Prof. Basant Mehta:* P.G. Dean,(Research), Prof. and Head, Department of Banking and Financial Management, Janardan Rai Nagar, Rajasthan Vidyapeeth University, Udaipur
2. *Prof. Rajeev Jain:* Director, Faculty of Management studies, J.R.N. Rajasthan Vidyapeeth University, Udaipur
3. *Prof. S. S. Sarangdevot:* Director, Deparment of Computer Science and Information Technology, JRN Rajasthan Vidyapeeth University, Udaipur
4. *Dr. Sarita Bhatnagar:* Asst. Prof. Faculty of Management Studies, JRN Rajasthan Vidyapeeth University, Udaipur
5. *Dr. Vikas Bhatnagar:* Asst. Prof. Vardhman Law Collage, Udaipur
6. *Dr. Tarun Shrimali:* Asst Prof. Department of Computer Science and Information Technolgy, JRN Rajasthan Vidyapeeth University, Udaipur
7. *Mr. Pawan Shanker Sharma:* Faculty, Aishwarya College, Udaipur
8. *Miss Ranjeeta Madhwani:* Faculty, Maharaja College of Management, Udaipur
9. *Miss Megashree Agarwal:* Faculty, Maharaja College of Management, Udaipur
10. *Mrs. Priyanka Choudhary:* Faculty, Cambay Institute of Hospitality Management, Udaipur
11. *Miss Kiran Vazirani:* Faculty, Pioneer Institute of Management, Udaipur
12. *Dr. (Mrs.) Shruti Kanthalia:* Senior Banker, Dubai
13. *Dr. Anurag Mehta*
14. *Dr. Hemant Somani*

Contents

SECTION–I
MARKETING MANAGEMENT

CHAPTER

1

Online Marketing : A Need to Face Marketing Challenges in the Globalized World

Prof. Basant Mehta
Miss Ranjeeta Madhwani

ABSTRACT

The world economy is becoming more 'regionalized' and more 'globalized'. The process of 'globalization' has been accompanied by the strengthening of economic and financial linkages within geographic regions. Global competition has been intensified with the introduction of new technologies. Those who can exploit the opportunities of this new technology will win. Internet marketing enables a large company to be responsive, innovative, and fast and a small company to compete internationally with the "big boys". Information technology changes on a month-to-month basis and sometimes week to week. The pace of change is accelerating. To remain competitive, companies must position themselves and commence marketing on the Internet. The article is intended to focus on various mistakes to be avoided while doing business online. It describes the online marketing tactics also. It deals with a marketer's thoughts on the use of Internet in their marketing endeavours and the global opportunities that now exist to be seized.

Keywords: *Online Marketing, Online Marketing Tactics, Online Marketing Mistakes, Steps to Success.*

Introduction

The advent of newer technologies and growth in IT industry has given more access points to Internet users. Use of the Internet as a consumer-oriented marketing tool has been common now over for five years and has become accepted as a standard marketing tool by the vast majority of businesses. Likewise, the Internet, email, and newsgroups are being widely used for business to business marketing programmes. As the use of Internet is increasing in leaps and bounds, companies are using their websites to sell their products and services directly to customers.

The rapid increase in the growth of online marketing can be attributed to many factors goods, services and ideas can move across continents efficiently at the click of a mouse. Anyone can link up with anyone else, anytime and anywhere in the world. With the advent of e-commerce, the rapid growth of the Internet and online transactions taking place at all times of the day night, today's markets, businesses and customers never sleep. This is not only a new challenge for global businesses attempting to serve a client base that spans time zones, but also for local enterprises that can no longer afford to restrict themselves to traditional hours of doing business. Online business is growing with assistance of new powerful technologies like satellite communication, mobile telecommunications, interactive voice recognition, data mining, digital signatures, virtual private networks, and portable computing. The aim of these technologies is to benefit a firm's online marketing efforts, in terms of both cost and value.

Online Marketing

E-commerce has redefined markets, industries and the way one does business. The growth of online marketing has just begun and it is at an early stage of evolution. The Internet has not only revolutionized personal lives, but has even transformed the world of business to a great extent. Every company today, irrespective of whether it is a dotcom company or not, has a presence on the net. The Internet has become an effective medium for reaching potential customers all over the globe.

Internet marketing is defined as "the use of Internet to advertise and sell merchandise or services." It involves the use of websites and e-mails to reach customers and inform them about the availability of a product, entertain their queries, and receive orders and payments through the electronic medium. Internet marketing is the component of marketing that deals with the planning, pricing, promotion, and distribution of products and services online. Good Internet marketing strategies clearly communicate a firm's unique selling proposition, or the unique collection of benefits that creates value for its customers.

Online marketing combines traditional marketing principles with the interactive capabilities of the Internet. The purpose of online marketing is to create awareness among customers about the offerings of the marketer, generate sales leads and get sales orders electronically. In online marketing, the tools used are e-commerce enabled websites, portals, e-newsletters, e-mails, e-catalogs, banner advertisements, e-marketplaces, etc. In online marketing, marketers devise plans to attract online visitors to a specific website and encourage them to register their names with them and/or purchase products.

The Benefits of Internet Marketing are:

- The Internet is the widest channel of communication available to small businesses. It can help level the playing field for small businesses on a limited budget that seek to compete in large markets. No other communications medium enables you to operate a business from your home, while giving a small business the appearance of a larger, more established operation.
- Marketing your product or service online offers the opportunity for increased communication with your

target market through techniques such as interactive websites, e-mail newsletters, online surveys and forms, blogs, and discussion groups. The Internet allows you to collect immediate feedback from your client base with little out-of-pocket expense.

- Print marketing materials and advertising strategies can be expensive to produce and traditionally have a short shelf life. Internet marketing techniques such as websites, banner ads and e-mail newsletters, can be produced at a reasonable cost, can contain more timely information than print brochures, and can be immediately and cost-effectively updated as your business changes.

Finding success online is no different from finding it offline. Choosing the right product or service and designing an appropriate online and offline marketing mix are key to successful Internet marketing.

Internet Marketing Tactics

There are many different technologies to facilitate Internet marketing strategy. Some of the most common and effective tools are as follows:

Search engines: A search engine is like a global yellow pages. There are over 850+ of these search engines around the world, however there are about 7 that are considered to get 90% of all Internet traffic. Some of the most popular search engines are Google, Alta Vista, WebCrawler, Infoseek, Lycos, Excite and Yahoo. Search engines help people find relevant information on the Internet. Major search engine maintain huge databases of websites that users can search by typing in keywords or phrases. Search engines are information gateways that have high traffic and are good for displaying advertisement/banners. They are used to find Internet information and for this reason, appeal to broad target groups.

AltaVista www.altavista.com	In theory, you should not have to register with AltaVista. The search engine should be able to find your site on its own, because it sends out crawlers that find sites and add them to AltaVista's index. The crawler follows links from other pages it finds, and that is how AltaVista adds more URLs to its index. So, if many pages are linked to your site, your site is more likely to be found. If not, it will never be found. To register, enter your URL in the form located at www.altavista .com/cgibin/query?pg=addurl. After this process is complete, AltaVista sends out crawlers to find the site, learn what is included in the content and add the URL to the index. Submission is free.
Lycos www.lycos.com	Lycos requires you to submit a URL for each page of your site, as well as your e-mail address. Lycos then sends a spider to your site. In approximately two to three weeks, your site will be entered into Lycos's catalog. Registration is free. If your site is not live for a certain amount of time, the spider cannot connect to it. Your site then gets deleted from the catalog.
Ask Jeeves www.ask.com	To submit a URL to Ask Jeeves' knowledge base, you send an e-mail including your URL and a short description of your site to Ask Jeeves. Human editors then review your request by visiting your site and checking if your site matches certain guidelines including quick loading time, regular updating of content and free

	features without the requirement of user registration. Ask Jeeves also uses its patented popularity search technology to determine which sites have provided the best answers to Ask Jeeves users. In addition to the previous guidelines, e-commerce sites should meet additional guidelines including security requirements, customer service and credibility as an e-commerce site.
Yahoo! www.yahoo.com	Before registering with Yahoo!, you should first check if your site is already in Yahoo's database. It is possible that your site has been suggested to Yahoo! by another user. If your site is in a foreign language, it may be located in an International Yahoo!. If it is in an International Yahoo! it will not be added to www.yahoo.com. Once you have determined that your site is not in Yahoo!, you should find an appropriate category in the Yahoo! directory to list your site. You can do this by going to the bottom of the category page and clicking on the link for suggesting a site. Yahoo! provides suggestions to help you determine where your site should be placed. Suggesting sites is free. To suggest a site using the normal process, you are only required to provide the name, URL and short description of the site. When using the Business Express you are required to pay a fee, guaranteeing that your site will be reviewed within seven business days.

GoogleSM www.google.com	Visit www.google.com/addurl.html to add a URL to Google. This search engine requests your URL and comments about your site (for Google's information), however it does not use the comments submitted for indexing purposes. Google does not index every site submitted. The engine only requires the submission of a site's main page because its crawler, Googlebot, will be able to find the rest of your pages as it searches all possible links. Google ranks pages by the number of connections between Web sites, with the theory that the more connections to a site, the more popular and useful the site. This is different compared to other search engines that use META tags and site descriptions as a method of ranking. Fig. 8.4 Search engines and their registration processes.
Search Engine Registration Requirements and Details	

E-Zines : (Online magzines) these publications are focuses on specific topics and may be a way to reach a target audience interested in that subject. Some companies have gathered the e-mail addresses of potential customers and used these lists to send out product information specific to client interests.

Benefits to establish an E-Zine

- Establish trust
- Brings visitors back
- Establishes you as an expert
- Keeps current and potential customers up to date on new products and services

- Builds relationships
- Allows you to build on Opt-In E-mail marketing list
- Keeps your website fresh in visitor's minds

Affiliate Marketing : Affiliate marketing enables to increase online sales by promoting products and services through a network of Affiliate sites on a payment-by-result basis. It also provides the opportunity to generate additional revenue by exploring site's own content to promote the products and services of other merchants. A merchant recruits content sites to partner with them as affiliates in exchange for commission. A common third party provider such as Commission Junction can be used. The merchant provides their advertising banners and links their Affiliates and assigns a commission for each click-through to their site, subscription to their service, or purchase of their products that is generated from those links. Affiliates place the tracking code for these ads and links on their Web sites. This allows click-through's to be tracked online and commission to be calculated. If a product or service is purchased, the customer pays the merchant directly and the affiliate is paid a commission for that transaction.

Banner Advertising : Banner advertising can play an extremely important role within website strategy. Banner advertising can be used as a means of promoting products, services, raising awareness, or as a way of generating revenue by selling advertising space on website.

- **Purchasing Advertising :** There are currently two widely recognized methods of purchasing banner advertising. The rates for these are usually quoted on a cost per thousand basis. The rates can vary tremendously as there is currently no standard price model.
- **Pay-Per-Impression :** This method of purchasing banner advertising is based on a charge for the number of times someone sees the banner. There are

no guarantees as to how many visitors will come to site as a result of seeing banner, the marketer is simply paying for the number of times his banner is displayed.

- **Pay-Per-Visitor** : this method of purchasing banner advertising is based on a charge for the number of times someone visits the site as a result of clicking on the banner. This is better method of purchasing banner advertising as the marketer is only paying for results, although expect to pay a premium.
- **Branding** : It creates brand awareness, and a brand image in the viewer's mind, whether or not the viewer clicks on the ad. Branding is very difficult to measure, but can be very powerful.

There are number of key issues that must be considered when designing a successful banner :

- It must have an attention grabbing headline.
- It must be simple and get your point across.
- It must invoke action (i.e. "click here").
- It must download quickly.
- It must be placed effectively on a website.

Common Online Marketing Mistakes

The online marketer should take steps to ensure that all communications used in different online marketing activities are consistent with the overall marketing communications strategy. Most *business* owners today recognize the importance of having a website. Like the telephone, it is a necessary tool that customers simply expect. It is also one of the most cost-effective ways to promote product or service locally, nationally or even internationally. But marketer may not realize however is that a bad website can actually cost his business rather than attract new customers. The following are some common mistakes and their solutions:

Using a Single "Doorway" For All Customers

Instead of using fancy, slow-loading Hash into movies a marketer should get real value from home page by using it to point prospects in the right direction. Many businesses serve multiple market segments, with an array of products that are applicable to one customer base but not necessarily the other. A website might already have inside pages that address each of their needs, but marketer should make it as easy as possible for his customers to find those pages. The idea is to use website's home page to guide visitors in the right direction rather than forcing them look for what is relevant to them. This is an easy way to improve their experience right from the start.

Poorly Written Webpage Copy

Webpage content should be clear, compelling, and concise and error free. Website's content is important because it builds trust and credibility with customers. Customers cannot see or interact with marketer in person, so they are relying on his website's content to be his representative, his salesperson. Poorly written copy with bad grammar and spelling mistakes equates to sleazy-looking or uninformed sales.

Missing or Mixed Sales Messages

It is estimated that over 60 per cent of online orders started are never actually followed through to completion. For Internet merchants, reducing their number of "abandoned" shopping carts is always a priority, and to do this they employ a number of proven sales techniques. One of these techniques is to continue sales messaging right through the entire checkout process. Many businesses do a great job of describing why their product or service is the best choice, only to present their customers with a sterile-looking checkout page. A multi-stage order form that asks for far more information is really a cause to close the sale. With nothing else to look at other than a product description, shipping fees and total price, buyers are left wondering if they have made the right choice. This is where many of them abandon their carts. Once content has convinced a prospect to place an order, it is important to reinforce in their minds that they have made a good decision. This can be done by reminding them about satisfaction guarantee, highlighting any discounts or incentives that are being applied to the order, with testimonials from existing clients and so on. Use every page of website, including the crucial order form pages, as an attentive salesperson to move the sale on to completion.

Hiding Customer Support Options

When it comes to buying online, studies show people are far less patient. But there is no reason to lose sales this way. A list of Frequently Asked Questions (FAQs) and their answers is great way to provide useful information. Also by including a contact page with a contact form, phone number, physical address and hours of operation can help customer in availing information. Finally, putting phone number at the top of every page to show customers that if they cannot find the information they are looking for online, help is only a phone call away.

Not Search Engine Optimizing Your Website

It is suggested to work with a reliable partner to develop an effective SEO (Search Engine Optimizing) strategy. Of all the Internet marketing options that are available to the marketer, search engine optimization (SEO) can have the greatest impact at attracting new business and keeping his business ahead of the competition. The purpose of SEO is to ensure that prospects find his business (instead of someone else's) when searching for the kinds of products or services he offer. SEO will help the marketer's website to rank highly (ideally on the first or second page) on related keyword searches. This is of critical importance because people rarely look past the 2nd page of results. Even if website is listed in a search engine's index, being on page 4, 5 or 50 of the search results will not do much good. The situation gets even worse if a competitor's website is ranked ahead. Achieving a good search engine ranking is done through a combination of specialized techniques. These include how Web pages are programmed, the content and formatting of each page, how website is structured and other factors.

Three Steps to Success

Successful marketing on the Internet is not just about advertising website in Google or buying banner ads on other websites. Without a quality product or service and a well developed website, a banner ad, for example, would do little good. To succeed online, a marketer must develop a comprehensive plan that includes the following:

1. A solid business model and great products or services
2. An effectively designed website with sales as an objective
3. An online marketing strategy that suits audience and fits budget

Conclusion

Online marketing has changed the way conventional marketing was being done. It has equipped marketers with the powerful tool of personalized communication. Marketers can reach out to individual customers and sell them just the products that they are looking for. Customers too are enjoying their new found power and are keen to exploit it to the fullest. They are becoming more and more demanding with each passing day and are actively communicating their expectations to the companies via the Internet. Most customers are willing to spend time browsing through company websites and chat rooms, etc. Now a marketer's success will be determined by his ability to utilize the information to reach out potential customers. To achieve success marketer should focus on various competent areas of success and avoid the common mistakes in online marketing.

REFERENCES

- Internet Marketing Secrets *Newsletter* November 14, 2008-Issue-149.
- 1CFAI Center for Management Research (2005), *"Marketing Management"*, pp. 411-425.
- Kumar Arun and N. Mecnakshi (2009), *"Marketing Management"*, Vikas Publication, pp. 573-594.
- Melody Y. Kiang (1999), T.S. Raghu and Kevin Huei Shang. *"Marketing on the Internet—Who Can Benefit from an Online Marketing Approach?"*
- P. Subba Rao (2008), *"International Business"*, Himalaya Publishing House, pp. 532-539.
- Sanjay Saxcna and Prabhat Chopra (2008), *"Computer Application in Management"* Vikas Publication, pp. 507-509.
- Vasudeva P.K. (2006), *"International Marketing"*, Excel Books, pp. 304-307.

WEBSITES

- www.globalmilleniamarketing.com
- www.wsi.com
- www.e-bc.ca

CHAPTER

2

Green Marketing : A Step to Improve Environmental Quality and Customer Satisfaction

Prof. Basant Mehta
Miss Ranjeeta Madhwani

ABSTRACT

Sustainability has become a global buzzword. There are obvious trends with automobiles, hotels, manufacturing, and other sectors that drive companies to promote anything they do that helps the environment. Although environmental issues influence all human activities, few academic disciplines have integrated green issues into their literature. This is especially true of marketing. As society becomes more concerned with the natural environment, businesses have begun to modify their behaviour in an attempt to address society's "new" concerns. Some businesses have been quick to accept concepts like environmental management systems and waste minimization, and have integrated environmental issues into all organizational activities. According to the American Marketing Association, green marketing is the marketing of products that are presumed to be environmentally safe. Thus green marketing incorporates a broad range of activities, including product modification, changes to the production process, packaging changes, as well as modifying advertising. The article deals with evolution of green concern and intends to focus on the concept of green marketing, its various issues, opportunities and challenges.

Keywords : *Green Marketing, Evolution, Issues, Opportunities, Challenges.*

Introduction

For the new century, the key challenge for mankind is to find more sustainable and equitable ways to produce, consume and live. The real challenge lies in turning these good intentions into meaningful progress in the face of powerful vested interests, a deeply entrenched and environmentally-hostile management paradigm, and a global economy with tremendous momentum on a trajectory which aims towards conventional economic growth. One business area where environmental issues have received a great deal of discussion in the popular and professional press is marketing.

Terms like "Green Marketing" and "Environmental Marketing" appear frequently in the popular press. Many governments around the world have become so concerned about green marketing activities that they have attempted to regulate them.

Evolution of Environmental Concept

The integration of environmental concern into marketing theory and practice is also viewed by some as simply an extension of the societal marketing concept. However, it is more helpful to view the concept of 'green marketing' which has developed as a response to the green movement of today, as something which integrates and expands upon the ideas embedded in the ecological and societal marketing concepts. The evolution of environmental concept can be seen in the following table.

In both the ecological and societal marketing concepts, the emphasis on socio-environmental issues for marketers has mostly been framed in terms of costs and constraints. Another important new dimension that green marketing introduced was an emphasis on socio-environmental issues as a potential source of innovation and opportunity for marketers. Combining environmental concern (which traditionally involves encouraging conservation), with the discipline of marketing (which aims to stimulate and facilitate consumption) can appear somewhat paradoxical.

The evolution of environmental concern

Factor	1970s environ-mentalism	1990s green
Emphasis	On 'environmental' problems	On the underlying problems with our social, economic, technical or legal systems
Geographic focus	On local problems (e.g. pollution)	On global issues (e.g. global warming)
Identity	Closely linked to other anti-establishment causes	A separate movement embraced by many elements of 'the establishment'
Source of support	An intellectual elite, and those at the fringes of society	A broad base
Basis of campaigns	Used forecasts of exponential growth to predict future environmental problems (e.g. limits to growth)	Uses evidence of current environmental degradation (e.g. the hole in the ozone layer)
Attitude to business	Business is the problem. Generally adversarial	Business seen as part of the solution. More partnerships formed.
Attitude to growth	Desire for zero grwoth	Desire for sustainable growth
View of environment/business interaction	Focussed on negative effects of business activity on the environment	Focuses on the dynamic interrelationship between business, society and the environment

Sustainability is the keystone of the green marketing philosophy, which resolves this apparent paradox. A sustainable approach to consumption and production involves enjoying a material standard of living today, which is not at the expense of the standard of living of future generations. It is a deceptively simple concept comprising two parts:

1. Using natural resources at a rate at which environmental systems or human activity can replenish them (or in the case of non-renewable resources, at a rate at which renewable alternatives can be substituted in).
2. Producing pollution and waste at a rate which can be absorbed by environmental systems without impairing their viability.

Green Marketing

Unfortunately, a majority of people believe that green marketing refers solely to the promotion or advertising of products with environmental characteristics. Terms like Phosphate Free, Recyclable, Refillable, Ozone Friendly, and Environmentally Friendly are some of the things consumers most often associate with green marketing. While these terms are green marketing claims, in general green marketing is a much broader concept, one that can be applied to consumer goods, industrial goods and even services. For example, around the world there are resorts that are beginning to promote themselves as "ecotourist" facilities, i.e., facilities that "specialize" in experiencing nature or operating in a fashion that minimizes their environmental impact [May 1991, Ingram and Durst 1989, Troumbis 1991].

According to the American Marketing Association, green marketing is the marketing of products that are presumed to be environmentally safe. Green marketing refers to the process of selling products and/or services based on their environmental benefits. Such a product or service may be environmentally friendly in itself or produced and/or packaged in an environmentally friendly way. Thus green marketing incorporates a broad range of activities, including product modification, changes to the production process, packaging changes, as well as modifying advertising. Yet defining green marketing is not a simple task. Indeed the terminology used in this area has varied, it includes: Green Marketing, Environmental Marketing and Ecological Marketing.

Green Marketing Issues

Various green marketing issues which a firm should integrate in its corporate culture are as follows:

Green Marketing and Social Responsibility

Many firms are beginning to realize that they are members of the wider community and therefore must behave in an environmentally responsible fashion. This translates into firms that believe they must achieve environmental objectives as well as profit related objectives. Finns in this situation can take two perspectives; 1) they can use the fact that they are environmentally responsible as a marketing tool; or 2) they can become responsible without promoting this fact. Walt Disney World (WDW) has an extensive waste management programme and infrastructure in place, yet these facilities are not highlighted in their general tourist promotional activities (Murphy 1985).

Governmental Pressure

As with all marketing related activities, governments want to "protect" consumers and society; this protection has significant green marketing implications. Governmental regulations relating to environmental marketing are designed to protect consumers in several ways: (1) reduce production of harmful goods or byproducts; (2) modify consumer and industry's use and/or consumption of harmful goods; or (3) ensure that all types of consumers have the ability to evaluate the environmental composition of goods. Governments establish regulations designed to control the amount of hazardous wastes produced by firms. Many by-products of production are controlled through the issuing of various environmental licences, thus modifying organizational behaviour. In some cases governments try to "induce" final consumers to become more responsible. For example, some governments have introduced voluntary curb-side recycling programmes, making it easier for consumers to act responsibly. In other cases governments tax individuals who act in an irresponsible fashion.

Competitive Pressure

Another major force in the environmental marketing area has been firms' desire to maintain their competitive position. In many cases firms observe competitors promoting their environmental behaviours and attempt to emulate this behaviour. In some instances this competitive pressure has caused an entire industry to modify and thus reduce its detrimental environmental behaviour. For example, it could be argued that Xerox's "Revive 100% Recycled paper" was introduced a few years ago in an attempt to address the introduction of recycled photocopier paper by other manufacturers. In another example when one tuna manufacture stopped using driftnets the others followed suit.

Cost or Profit Issues

Firms may also use green marketing in an attempt to address cost or profit related issues. Disposing of environmentally harmful by-products, such as polychlorinated biphenyl (PCB) contaminated oil are becoming increasingly costly and in some cases difficult. Therefore firms that can reduce harmful wastes may incur substantial cost savings. When attempting to minimize waste, firms are often forced to re-examine their production processes. In these cases they often develop more effective production processes that not only reduce waste, but reduce the need for some raw materials. This serves as a double cost savings, since both waste and raw materials are reduced. In other cases firms attempt to find end-of-pipe solutions, instead of minimizing waste. In these situations firms try to find markets or uses for their waste materials, where one firm's waste becomes another firm's input of production. One Australian example of this is a firm who produces acidic waste water as a byproduct of production and sells it to a firm involved in neutralizing base materials. The last way in which cost or profit issues may affect firms' environmental marketing activities is that new industries may be developed. This can occur in two ways: 1) a firm develops a technology for reducing waste and sells it to other firms; or 2) a waste recycling or removal industry develops.

Opportunities

All types of consumers, both individual and industrial are becoming more concerned and aware about the natural environment. In a 1992 study of 16 countries, more than *50%* of consumers in each country, other than Singapore, indicated they were concerned about the environment. A 1994 study in Australia found that 84.6% of the sample believed all individuals had a responsibility to care for the environment. A further 80% of this sample indicated that they had modified their behaviour, including their purchasing behaviour, due to environmental reasons. As demands change, many firms see these changes as an opportunity to be exploited. It can be assumed that firms marketing goods with environmental characteristics will have a competitive advantage over firms marketing non-environmentally responsible alternatives. There are numerous examples of firms who have strived to become more environmentally responsible, in an attempt to better satisfy their consumer need. McDonald's replaced its clam shell packaging with waxed paper because of increased consumer concern relating to polystyrene production and Ozone depletion.

Challenges

For marketing, the challenge is two-fold. In the short term, ecological and social issues have become significant external influences on companies and the markets within which they operate. Companies have to react to changing customer needs, new regulations and a concern about the socio-environmental impacts of business. In the longer term, the pursuit of sustainability will demand fundamental changes to the management paradigm which underpins marketing and the other business functions.

There are a number of potential problems that must overcome. One of the main problems is that firms using green marketing must ensure that their activities are not misleading to consumers or industry, and do not breach any of the regulations or laws dealing with environmental marketing. Green marketing claims must clearly state environmental benefits. A problem of the firms face is that those who modify their products due to increased consumer concern must contend with the fact that consumers' perceptions are sometimes not correct. Some firms, like Coca-Cola and Walt Disney World, are becoming socially responsible without publicizing the point. They may be protecting themselves from potential future negative backlash; if it is determined they made the wrong decision in the past. While governmental regulation is designed to give consumers the opportunity to make better decisions or to motivate them to be more environmentally responsible, there is difficulty in establishing policies that will address all environmental issues.

The push to reduce costs or increase profits may not force firms to address the important issue of environmental degradation. End-of-pipe solutions may not actually reduce the waste but rather shift it around. While this may be beneficial, it does not necessarily address the larger environmental problem, though it may minimize its short term affects. Ultimately most waste produced will enter the waste stream, therefore to be environmentally responsible organizations should attempt to minimize their waste, rather than find "appropriate" uses for it.

Conclusion

Green marketing will not only be making a positive impact on the local community and environment but also be increasing profits by lowering energy costs. Customers will support such a company with their repeat business. However there are various challenges before a company adopting green marketing concept in its business. The lack of consideration of the true "greenness" of activities may result in firms making false or misleading green marketing claims. Firms should integrate environmental issues in its corporate culture. They should also realize that they are members of the wider community and must behave in environmentally responsible fashion so as to achieve environmental objectives as well as profit related objectives.

REFERENCES

- Ingram, C. Denise and Patrick B. Durst. 1989. "Nature-oriented Tour Operators: Travel to Developing Countries." *Journal of Travel Research* 28 (2): 11-18.
- Jain K. Sanjay. (2004), "Green Marketing: An Attitudinal and Behavioural Analysis of Indian Consumers", *Global Business Review,* Vol. 5, No. 2, 187-205.
- Murphy, P. (1985), *"Tourism: A Community Approach",* New York: Methuen Inc.
- Nayar. (2008). *Green Marketing—New Hopes and Challenges,* retrieved from: http://www. 123 eng.com.
- Ottman, J.A. (1993), "Green Marketing: Challenges and opportunities", *NTC Business Books,* Chicago, IL.
- Polonsky, Michael Jay. (1994). "An Introduction To Green Marketing", *Electronic Green Journal,* 1(2), retrieved from: http://www.escholarship.org/uc/item/49n325b7.

WEBSITES

- www.heldref.org/env.php
- www.about.com
- www.wikipedia.com

CHAPTER

3

Impact of Recession on Indian Organized Retail

Prof. Basant Mehta
Ms. Kiran Vazirani

Introduction

The word retail is derived from the French word *'Retaillier'* meaning to cut a piece off or to break bulk. Retailing includes all the activities involved in selling goods or services directly to final consumers for personal, non-business use. A retailer or retail store is any business enterprise whose sales volume comes primarily from retailing. Any organization selling to final consumers (including final consumption by manufacturers, distributors, etc.) is doing retailing (Kotler and Keller, 2006). Retailing involves a direct interface with the customers and the coordination of business activities from end to end, including delivery and post delivery service to the customers (Vedmani G G, 2008).

Retail business can be clearly demarcated into: Organized and Unorganized. Organized retailing is still evolving in India, with its share being only 4 per cent of total retailing. The organized retailing has hit hard by recession, due to various problems, like drop in consumer spending and shift from leisure to value based purchases. The change in consumer spending pattern has also had an adverse impact on shopping malls, with footfall declining and with every major player trying out new strategies to sail through this downslide. Retail business contributes nearly 10 per cent to India's GDP. India also has the largest number of retailers, about 12 million though they are mostly small (Bajaj Cheta, 2005). According to AT Kearney, around 7 per cent of the population in India is engaged in retailing.

Overview of Retailing in India

Retailing in India has evolved from traditional *haats, mandis* and *melas* to modern formats like hypermarkets, departmental stores, and malls. All these retail formats exists, demonstrating the uniqueness of the Indian market in accepting both the traditional and the modern.

Though there are 12 million retail outlets in India, most of them are less than 500 sq. ft in size. The per capita retailing space is thus one of the lowest in the world. The retail business in India during the year 2007 amounted to $ 385 bn, and a McKinsey study says that this is estimated to $ 1.52tn by 2025.

India Retail Market Statistics

- 720 million Indians to join consuming age by 2010.
- 55 per cent of the Indian population will be under 20 years of the age by 2015.
- 32 per cent rise in urbanization by 2008.
- 10 per cent annual growth in retail market since 2000.
- 7 per cent of the population is engaged in retailing.
- A booming US $300 billion retail market in India.
- 5.5 retail outlets per 1000 population, highest in the world.
- 25-30 per cent annual growth in retail loans and credit cards.

Organized Retailing : Advantages to Indian Economy

- Organized retail will result in a complete revamp of the agricultural supply chain in the country. A recent study by CRISIL has estimated a current annual total loss of about Rs. 1000 billion in the agricultural supply chain, 57 per cent of which is due to avoidable wastage and the rest due to the avoidable costs of storage and commissions (CRISIL Research, June 2007). Organized retailers have already started procuring fruit and vegetables from farmers directly by passing the various intermediaries who add more costs than value to the food chain. They are investing heavily on logistics in th form of centralized warehousing and distribution centers, transport and cold storage, either directly or through engaging third part logistics companies.

- Boost to Exports: Some of the international retailers that have plans for India in the future have already developed suppliers in the country and have started exporting from India. For example, Wal Mart exported an equivalent of US $600 million, and IKEA about 380 million Euros from India in 2006-07.
- Organized retailing will work with farmers to: (1) improve yields by enabling them to obtain quality input supplies; (2) adopt superior farm technology and practices; and (3) access timely credit at reasonable rates.
- Small scale manufacturers will be the major beneficiaries of private labels.
- Organized retail's direct purchase from farmers and other suppliers compresses the supply chain and eliminates a large number of intermediaries and hence can offer consumers a lower price than the traditional channels.
- Unorganized retailers normally do not pay taxes and most of them are not even registered for sales tax, VAT, or income tax. Organized retailers, by contrast, are corporate entities and hence file tax returns regularly.

Slowdown Impacts Retailers

Retailers face a sharp decline in their sales as a result of the current economic uncertainty. Sales in the metros have witnessed substantial slowdown, which is reflected in the quarterly sales figures. The operating costs of retailers remain high, leading to the decline in profit in profit margins (*refer Exhibit. 1*).

Exhibit 1: Deteriorating Numbers in Apparel Retailing

	Sales Growth (%)	Profit Growth (%)
	Y–O–Y	Y–O–Y
Celebrity Fashions	–25	*
Kutons Retail	32	7
Pantaloon Retail	24	6
Shopper's Stop	9	*
Vishal Retail	24	–86
Trent	–15	–43
Kewal Kiran	–18	–40
Provogue	1	–10
Indiabulls Retail	–73	*
The company incurred loss		
Source: The Hindu, Business Line, February 06, 2009.		

The figures shown in *Exhibit 1* are on a year-on-year basis for the quarter ending December 31, 2008. In the face of the aforementioned problems, retailers need not to only think of immediate survival, but also increase their return on investment through possible improvements in their fundamentals and by exploiting potential untapped areas.

Literature Review

According to Kumar Rajagopalan, the CEO of Retailers Association of India, the impact of global recession is likely to be felt for 12 to 18 more months. Most retailers have their business model focussed on the middle income class, who are significantly affected by this recessionary trend. It will, therefore, be difficult to handle recession without new marketing initiatives and better price offerings.

"Indian Retail: Time to Change Lanes", a report by the global consultancy firm KPMG states that the ongoing recession has taken a major toll on the dissemination of India's organized retail, with the retail sector's sales growth falling drastically to 4 per cent in December 2008 from the corresponding previous year's figure of 34 per cent. The share of the organized retail sector, which was earlier projected to touch 16 per cent by 2012 from the current 5 per cent, is likely to reach around 10 per cent. Investment flow in organized retailing in India, which was projected at around $25 bn over the next four to five years, is also slowing down. The KPMG national; industry director Ramesh Srinivas said (KPMG Report, 2009) that slowing sales and increasing working capital requirements to fuel growth have resulted in liquidity pressures for many domestics' retailers. According to the Cartesian Economic Meltdown Survey of December 2008, the retail sector has come under a moderate impact of slowdown; and the retailers are facing the double impact of falling footfalls and poor conversion ratio.

The *'Images Retail'* Magazine, in its article on retailing during recession deals with the problem of consumer spending. It reports that of consumer spending stagnated since 2008, resulting in barely any sale growth. It tries to identify three important actions required to survive, i.e., generate cash, strengthen trust of customers and communicate with employees and other business associates. Ambeek Kheka, Group President, Vishal Retail is reported to have said, "Sales have been affected, but we still have to evaluate the degree. There are heavy discounts and 'buy one get one free' schemes. We are selling some products even at negligible margins."

In a deteriorating macroeconomic climate, retailers may be forced to give discounts and promotional offers to maintain volumes, which will drive down the margins.

According to the Indian Retail Sector Outlook 2009 by Fitch Research, the Indian retail industry has been affected over by various factors, including slow economic growth, high interest rates and liquidity crunch. The industry was also affected by the high cost of real estate rents during 2008, although this eased to some extent during 2009. Most retailers experienced a drop in footfall and demand, reflecting in slowing store sales and in a greater time to break even. Same store sales were lower in 2009 due to slow Indian GDP growth.

"Retailers Choose Rental Antidote to Beat Recession "by Dam M (2009), states that falling footfalls and poor conversion ratio led to a decline in sales growth to 11 per cent in December 2008, as compared to 35 per cent in December 2007. Big retailers like the Future Group, Reliance and Aditya Brila Retail were renegotiating rentals to bring down costs.

The crisis in consumer confidence and discretionary purchases has had a major effect on retail strategies. Future Group has shut down 20 smaller warehouses and consolidated them into bigger areas up to 2.5 lacs sq. ft. RPG Retail and Shoppers have also implemented automatic replenishment system which enables them to track stock movement at the store level. RPG Retail has tied up with vendors to enable direct supply to some of their big Spencer's stores, instead of routing them through a warehouse so as to reduce costs. Fearing the current economic meltdown, Wadhawan Food Retail Pvt. Ltd has put its plan to launch hypermarkets on hold. It has also closed 18 of its 20 grocery stores, which include Spinach, S-mart and Sabka Bazaar.

In India's Retail Sector: Time to Take Stock, Fifer and Padmanabhan state that players like RPG's Spencer's Retail, Videocon's Next and India Bulls Retail, all began with much promise, but are today struggling to keep afloat. Reliance Retail is reducing headcount and Aditya Birla Retail has pruned its growth plans. Some of the big players are now taking time out to study the market closely and relook their strategies. Reliance, which believed in doing it alone, is now partnering with niche brands and has tied up with niche brands and tied up for supply chain and infrastructure development. Spencer's Retail and Big Bazaar have shifted focus from food and grocery business to high yielding fashion apparel. Cutting down on operating costs is high on the agenda as well. Lease rental are being renegotiated. There is an attempt to rationalize salaries and control electricity expenses.

According to an article in *retailmantra.com,* the Indian economic slowdown is now pinching the pockets of retailers more than ever. Reliance Retail is all set to position itself as a "value retailer" to drive footfalls and improve its performance. Provogue in Mumbai had to be satisfied with 20 per cent less sales last Christmas. And Lee used gift vouchers to promote sales.

Hence, it is clear from these articles and reports that Indian retail has not escaped the impact of the recession and organized retailers have been trying to deal with the situation.

India's Retail Journey in Recession : (Some Statistics)

- **Declined Penetration:** Where the Q3 growth numbers of FY 2008-09 at 10-12 per cent as against 35 per cent of the previous year, the 'happy grins' are fast turning into 'nervous smiles', while the sector is still registering decent growth, the heavy investments made during the boom period may weigh the retailers down.

Organized Retail Penetration—Gap Created by Slowdown

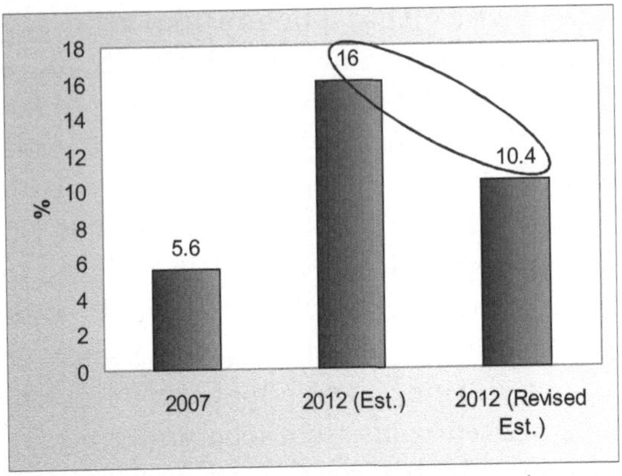

Organized retail penetration, which was expected to touch 16 per cent by 2012 from the current 5 per cent, is likely to trace 10.4 per cent only

Source: KPMG Analysis and Retailers Association of India

Organized retail penetration, which was expected to touch 16 per cent by 2012 from current 5 per cent, is likely to trace 10.4 per cent only.

- **Disappointing Footfalls:** According to KPMG's survey, 70 per cent of the respondents stated that the slowdown has adversely affected their footfalls.

Year-on-Year Net Sales Growth

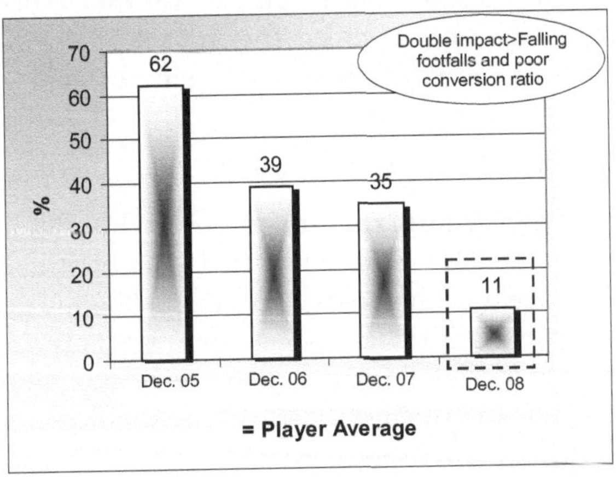

- **Liquidity under pressure :** The slowing sales are resulting in lower inventory turnover and increasing working capital requirements for retailers. This in turn has resulted in liquidity pressures for many retailers. To free the cash that has been locked, a large number of companies have been trying to reduce the inventory on their books and shorten working capital cycles.

Working Capital on the rise

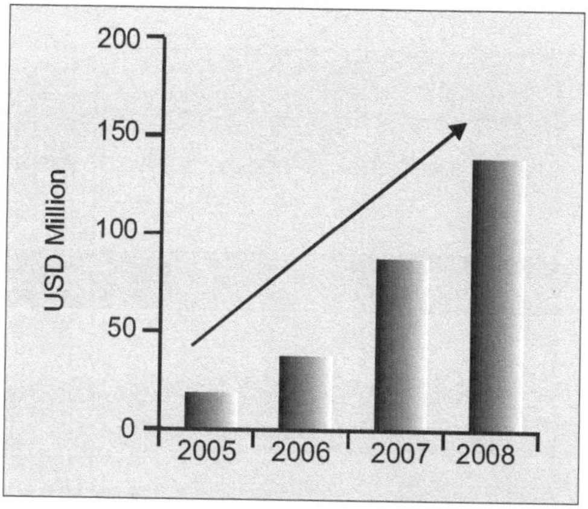

Decline in Inventory Turnover

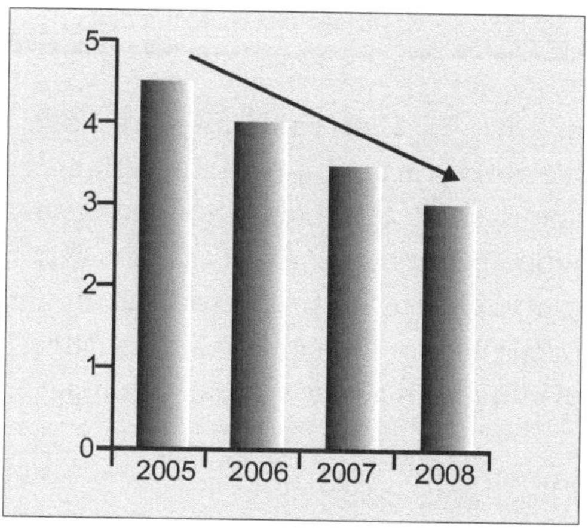

- **Rentals-skyrocketing to all time high :** Because of the economic slowdown, many retail stores are shutting shops—high rentals, coupled with low returns and mounting interest rates, made once successful Shubhiksha close 1200 stores across India. Reliance shut around 50 of its Reliance Fresh stores and lay off 13 per cent of its 30,000 strong workforce.

Rentals eating into profit margin of retailers

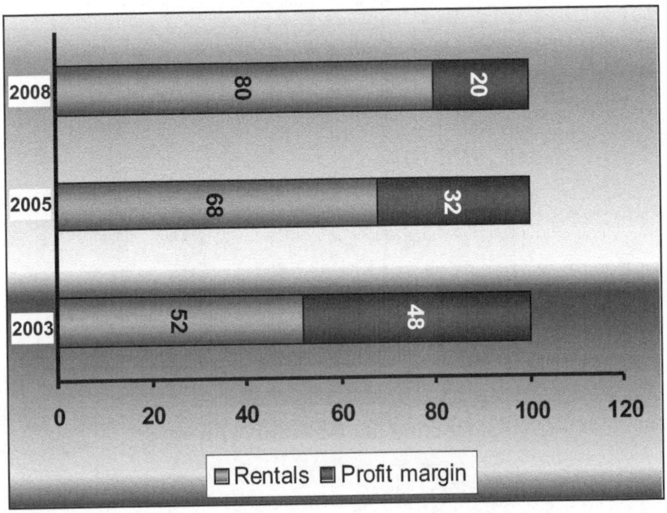

- **Margin Contraction—Interest burden adversely impacts profits :** Besides the weak economy and the feeble consumer sentiments, the disappointing retail growth is also attributed to poor supply chain management and weak support infrastructure, absence of a mature 3 PL player providing high service levels at competitive prices.

Net Profit Margin

Cost containment to maintain margins proved successful

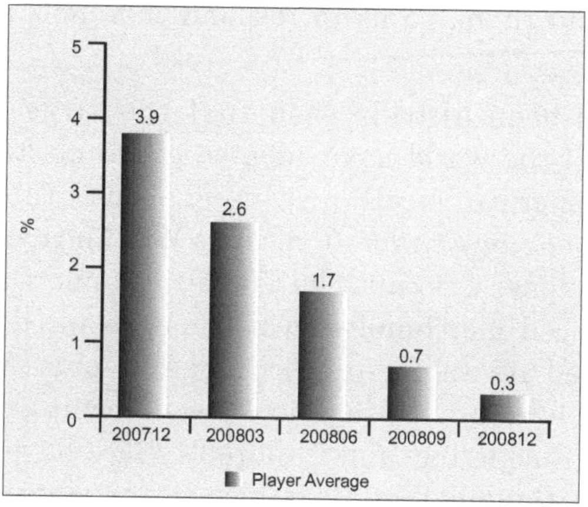

Operating Profit Margin

But high leverage and fixed finance cost led to PAT margin contraction

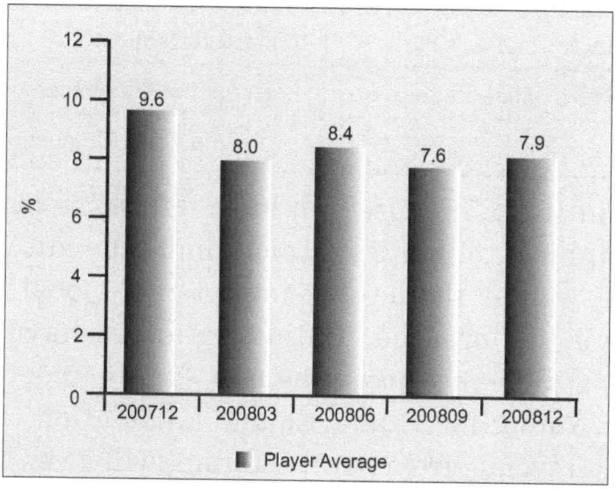

Strategies Followed by Different Retailers in India

In this section, we take a look at the different strategies opted by retailers in India as well as the other options available to them, so as to respond this global economic slowdown.

It has been already seen that the large organized retailers of the world have adopted different strategies so that customer can recall their brand even at this economic slowdown (*Refer Exhibit 4*). Such as Wal-Mart is opting for price uniqueness. Because he thinks, customers stocked up on low-priced merchandise which has resulted Wal-Mart quadrupled its same-store-sales gains over May 2007. Discount club Costco also posted a significant gain at 4 per cent. But Buckle Inc. and Children's Place have explained that even though Wal-Mart has better clothing prices, consumers went for better clothing style. This demonstrates irrefutably that a "Product USP" has power even in tight economy.

Exhibit 4 : Strategies followed by different retailers of the world

Companies	Strategies
Wal-Mart & Costco	Price Uniqueness
Buckle Inc. & Children's Place	Product Uniqueness
Staples, NOT Office Depot	Experience Uniqueness
Exxon & Mobil	Unremarkable Uniqueness

But in India, because of a huge difference in cultural, demographical, climatic, income and expenditure ratio, social, as well as the level of impact that global economic slowdown has created, Indian retailers have to plan something different. According to a survey undertaken by Ernst & Young for Brand Equity Foundation (IBEF) in 2007, the revenue from rural retailing will grow by 60 per cent till 2012, in which maximum share of demand would come from consumer and household products. Many organized retail chains are moving towards the Tier II and Tier III cities with their own formats and strategies (*Refer Exhibit 5*). Already, giants like Indian Tobacco Company (ITC), DCM Sriram Consolidated Ltd. (DSCL), Godrej (Godrej Aadhar) and many others, have rolled out their unique retailing formats for rural areas. ITC's coupal Saga and DCM's Hariyali Kisan Bazaar, HUL's Shakti, Reliance Retail, etc., are rubbing shoulders with rural masses to strike an emotional connect with them. These giants are creating employment opportunities and income for the people in the rural areas through their retailing models.

Exhibit 5 : Organized Retailers of India-Geographical shift towards Smaller cities

Companies	Strategies	Reasons
Reliance Retail	Franchise Model	Real Estate pressures
Trent(Westside)	Franchise Model	Real Estate pressures
Vishal Retail	Expanding in Tier II and Tier III cities	Declining profits in Metro and Tier I cities
Raymond	Franchise mode of expansion in Tier II and Tier III cities	Falling footfalls and declining in demand in Tier I cities
Brand House Retail (Manages S Kumars Brands)	Franchise mode of expansion in Tier II and Tier III cities	Falling footfalls and declining in demand in Tier I cities

Source: *The Economic Times, December 22, 2008.*

Options Available to Them

Following are the options available to the organized retailers so as to beat the current economic slowdown and come up as successful organizations:

(1) **Increase Retail Loyalty:** For the retailers, it is important to provide consumers with the right kind of product at the right price and thus, inculcate brand loyalty. Retail therapy works because by looking at the brand with which one has been associated for long, the customer can recollect the good times.

(2) **Innovative Customer Relationship Management (CRM):** Innovative CRM activities are the need of the hour along with different product ranges catering to the changing needs of the customers. Value for money products will sell, as the customer is now looking for the long-term investments and not just short-term delight, as was the case earlier.

(3) **Value through Effective Supply Chains:** Efficient supply chain with integration (both vertical and horizontal) in the supply chain by the retailers is a possibility, in which profit margins will increase and customers too can benefit with low prices.

(4) **Disintermediation Strategy:** Disintermediation in retail should be attempted at all levels during economic slowdown. Bypassing the distributors, suppliers or Original Equipment Manufacturers (OEMs) is referred to as disintermediation. This can benefit them by forming an association for negotiating with the manufacturers for bulk purchases and price discounts.

(5) To counter this declining sale, the organized retailers take up private labels business more aggressively as the new mantra to beat the slowdown. This will enable them to leverage the benefits of branded products, while keeping the prices lower and more cost effective for consumers, rather than the corresponding national brands. Private labels offer better value for money to the consumers.

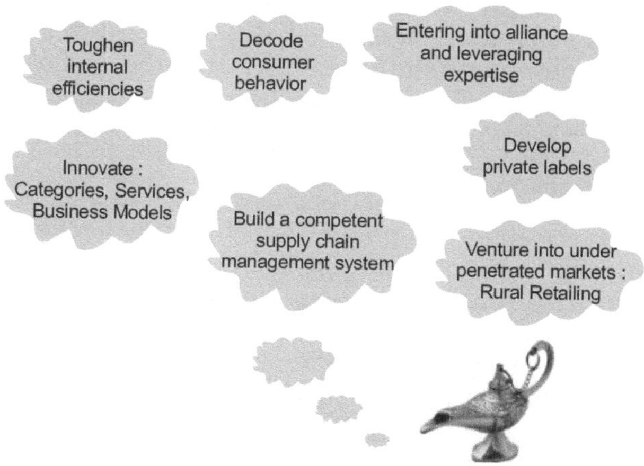

(6) It is the time to enter into alliances or partnerships, manage stores more effectively, take help from experts and change the product profiles to match customer needs. Diversify and move towards the nicher rather than mass markets. Renegotiate rental and improve backend operations through effective inventory management and cost cutting techniques.

(7) **Effective Sales Promotions:** John Wanamaker, an American merchant, was once quoted as saying that 50 per cent of advertising expenditure is wasted away," though he himself admitted that he did not know which 50 per cent was wasted. But going by traditional mass marketing and communication, the above statement seems to be very appropriate. When marketers complain of attention scarcity, advertising clutter and communication without direction, it is very much natural to be inclined towards sales promotion activities which can promote sales and generate loyalty.

(8) **Future Store Technologies and Efficiencies:** The use of information technology can bring in a lot of efficiency in the supply chain by connecting and collaborating retailers, distributors and manufacturers. However, Radio Frequency Identification (RFID) technology has tremendous potential for use in the retail sector. Global giants, like Wal-Mart, Tesco and Carrefour, have used RFID as an integral part of their operating process. But in India, so far mainly the Future Group and Reliance Retail have shown inclination partial use of RFID in their operations.

Conclusion

However, the India Shopping Center Forum 2009 ended on a positive note, where it was stated that there are immense opportunities and possibilities for mall developers and retailers to explore beyond metros. The growing consumer needs in the mini metros, Tier II and Tier III cities are almost matching up to that in the metros.

Moreover, most retailers are trying to improve efficiency by reducing inventories, improving back-end management, renegotiating lease rentals and even asking the government to allow more FDI presence in this sector.

Thus it seems that this sector will recover and get back on the tract, in spite of the effects of the economic slowdown. One must remember that customers never stop coming to retail stores during recession. Rather, their purchases decrease because of the retailer's recessionary approach towards them.

BIBLIOGRAPHY

Websites

www.retailindustry.about.com
www.retailmantra.com
www.pantaloon.com

Books

1. Marketing Management by Philip Kotler.
2. Retailing Management—Text and Cases by Swapna Pradhan.

Magazines and Press Sources

Business Today
Business World—The Marketing White Book, 2008
Marketing Mastermind—September, December-2009.
KPMG Consumer Reports—Indian Retails, Time to Change Lames, 2009
Economic Times
Business Standard

CHAPTER

4

Rural Vs. Globalized Market : Rural Market Booming with Business Prospectus

Prof. Basant Mehta
Miss Meghashree Agarwal

ABSTRACT

In this era of globalization, the changing demography, economy and social environment of "Rural India" are making an indication towards the optimal sphere for the business organization. The rural market has a grip of strong country shops, which affect the sale of various products in rural market. The companies are trying to trigger growth in rural areas. They are identifying the fact that rural people are now in the better position with disposable income. The low rate finance availability has also increased the affordability of purchasing the costly products by the rural people. Marketer should understand the price sensitivity of a consumer in a rural area. This paper is therefore an attempt to promote the rural market in India. Rural marketing is the strategic approach adopted by so many big players from the Indian origin to target MNCs. such as HUL, LG, Samsung, Revlon and insurance biggies like Birla Sunlife, Max New York Life and Prulife in the era of globalization to cope up with tremendous competition.

Keywords: *Rural marker in Indian economy, Impact of globalization in developing countries and India, India's rural innovation, Rural India: Glitter in times of gloom, Strategies for rural marketing, Potential sectors of rural markets, Challenges of rural marketing.*

Background

Three-quarters of the world's 1.2 billion poor people live in rural areas. The majority are still small-scale producers who depend on agriculture and natural resources for their livelihoods. International markets have been seen as a way out of poverty and food insecurity for small-scale producers. These markets comprise traditional food and fiber commodities, but also new markets for quality products, biodiversity conservation, and mitigation of climate change. Increasing volatility and severe requirements in these markets, as well as international trade agreements, present small holders and their organizations with multiple opportunities and risks. Higher value has to be weighed against the costs of meeting international standards and certification for quality products and the imbalance of market power when trading with large companies. Imports markets can exclude small producers from their home markets.

Rural India with its traditional perceptions has grown up over the years, not only in terms of income, but also in terms of thinking. The rural markets are growing at about two time faster pace than urban markets, not surprisingly, rural India accounts for 60 per cent of the total national demand. Rural India with a population of 630 million (approximately) would become bigger than total consumer market in countries such as South Korea or Canada in another 20 years and it will grow at least four times from its existing size.

Rural Markets are defined as those segments of overall market of any economy, which are distinct from the other types of markets like stock market, commodity markets or Labour economics. Rural Markets constitute an important segment of overall economy, for example, in the USA, out of about 3000 countries, around 2000 counties are rural, that is, non-urbanized, with population of 55 million. Typically, a rural market will represent a community in a rural area with a population of 2500 to 30000.The intricacies of rural marketing and their implication for economic progress have often been underestimated at significant cost of the economic development.

Rural Marketing in Indian Economy

The concept of *Rural Marketing in Indian Economy* has always played an influential role in the lives of people. In India, leaving out a few metropolitan cities, all the districts and industrial townships are connected with rural markets. The rural market in India is not a separate entity in itself and it is highly influenced by the sociological and behavioural factors operating in the country. The rural population in India accounts for around 627 million, which is exactly 74.3 percent of the total population. The rural market in India brings in bigger revenues in the country, as the rural regions comprise of the maximum consumers in this country. The rural market in Indian economy generates almost more than half of the country's income. Rural marketing in Indian economy can be classified under two broad categories. These are:

- The market for consumer goods that comprise of both durable and non-durable goods.
- The market for agricultural inputs that include fertilizers, pesticides, seeds, and so on.

However, rural marketing determines the carrying out of business activities bringing in the flow of goods from urban sectors to the rural regions of the country as well as the marketing of various products manufactured by the non-agricultural workers from rural to urban areas. To be precise, Rural Marketing in Indian Economy covers two broad sections, namely:

- Selling of agricultural items in the urban areas
- Selling of manufactured products in the rural regions

The steps taken by the Government of India to initiate proper irrigation, infrastructural developments, prevention of flood, grants for fertilizers, and various schemes to cut down the poverty line have improved the condition of the rural masses. Of course it is a huge market particularly for the consumer goods, durables and farm inputs, and services. Rural incomes are rising and with television, internet and mobiles it is opening up quite speedily.

Impact of Globalization on Developing Countries and India

Globalisation is the new buzzword that has come to dominate the world since the nineties of the last century with the end of the cold war and the break-up of the former Soviet Union and the global trend towards the rolling ball. Globalisation has brought in new opportunities to developing countries. Greater access to developed country markets and technology transfer hold out promise improved productivity and higher living standard. But globalisation has also thrown up new challenges like growing inequality across and within nations, volatility in financial market and environmental deteriorations. Another negative aspect of globalisation is that a great majority of developing countries remain removed from the process. Till the nineties the process of globalisation of the Indian economy was constrained by the barriers to trade and investment liberalisation of trade, investment and financial flows initiated in the nineties has progressively lowered the barriers to competition and has tended the pace of globalisation.

Globalization, the economic integration in trade, investment and finance, takes the form of liberalization, privatization and deregulation. In developing and under-developed countries, however, globalization translates into corporate dominance over local enterprises and of international capital over domestic economies. Corporate monopolies dominate the ownership structures of local economies and the organization of production methods. They have control over technology, raw material sourcing and access to markets. Meanwhile the globalization process continues to dismantle policies and regulations safeguarding the rights of people, their health, environment and livelihoods that are perceived by neo-liberal pundits as "protectionism". Globalization is also reducing public expenditure on social services, such as health and education, by governments and shifting control of these services to corporations. Due to globalization and the need to seek out new markets, rural marketing is gaining new importance in India as well as across the globe.

India's Rural Innovations

In recent years, rural markets have acquired significance in countries like China and India, as the overall growth of the economy has resulted into substantial increase in the purchasing power of the rural communities. On account of the green revolution in India, the rural areas are consuming a large quantity of industrial and urban manufactured products. In this context, a special marketing strategy, namely, *rural marketing* has taken shape. Sometimes, *rural marketing* is confused with *agricultural marketing*—the later denotes marketing of produce of the rural areas to the urban consumers or industrial consumers, whereas rural marketing involves delivering manufactured or processed inputs or services to rural producers or consumers. Also, when we consider the scenario of India, there is a picture that comes out, huge market for the developed products as well as the labor support. This has led to the change in the mindset of the marketers to move to these parts of the world.

Also rural market is getting an importance because of the saturation of the urban market. As due to the competition in the urban market, the market is more than or as saturated as most of the capacity of the purchasers has been targeted by the marketers. So the marketers are looking for extending their product categories to an unexplored market i.e. the rural market. This has also led to the CSR activities being done by the corporate to help the poor people attain some wealth to spend on their product categories. Here we can think of HLL (now, HUL) initiatives in the rural India. One of such project is the *Project Shakti,* which is not only helping their company attain some revenue but also helping the poor women of the village to attain some money which is surely going to increase their purchasing power. Also this will increase their brand loyalty as well as recognition in that area. A mother of two who was left to fend for her and two daughters after her husband abandoned the family, Rojamma initially made ends meet by working in her parents' fields. Then she joined the Shakti project and became a distributor of Hindustan Lever products. The commission Rojamma earned on her sales helped provide income for her family. "The lives of thousands of women have changed because of Shakti."

Similarly we can think of the *ITC E-Chaupal,* which is helping the poor farmers get all the information about the weather as well as the market price of the foodgrains they are producing. In other view these activities are also helping the companies increase their brand value. So as it is given above the significance of the rural market has increased due to the saturation of the urban market as well as in such conditions the company which will lead the way will be benefited as shown by the success of HUL and ITC initiatives. "While the E-Choupal network was initiated to facilitate more efficient and effective procurement, the connectivity—both physical and informational—between the farmer and the market that it facilitated has allowed ITC to use it for distribution of goods and services from the market to the farmer".

The FMCG sector includes companies like Indian Tobacco Corporation (ITC), Godrej, Hindustan Lever Limited (HLL), Gujarat Cooperative Milk Marketing Federation (GCMMF-Amul) and Dabur India Limited. All these have shown a strong global presence in the rural sector and it can be said that all the FMCG companies should target the rural sector.

Some FMCGs products like toothpaste, hair oil and other like shampoos have done much better in the rural areas than the urban and the semi urban areas. It has been a phenomenon that the sales of many companies have gone up; Coca-Cola, Nestle and Godrej too have also reported better sales in rural areas.

Rural India : Glitter in Times of Gloom

No company can afford to ignore two third of the consumer population pie. However inaccessible they may be and whatever changes may be required in the company's strategy to attract them. No wonder, the growing power of the rural consumer (accounting for 64% of country's total consumer base) is forcing Indian blue chips and MNCs to flock to rural markets. 70% of India's and 12% of globe's population lives in rural India and contributes 50% of country's GDP. In fact, despite rising urbanization, 63% of India's population will continue to live in the rural areas even in 2025.

Surging Ahead in Terms of Growth

As per National Council of Applied Economic Research (NCAER), rural market accounts for 55% of LIC policies, 70% of toilet soap consumption, and 50% of TV, fans, bicycles, tea and wrist watch consumption. So as a target market, it is attractive not only because of the size, but also because of impressive growth potential.

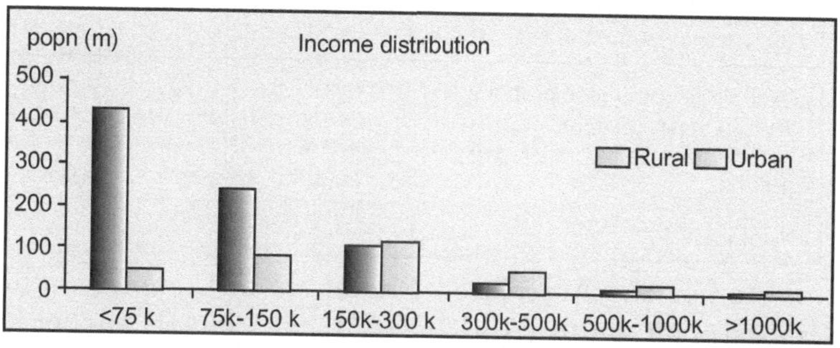

Rural GDP has been witnessing strong growth in the last four years (average of 4%) not only on the back of increase in minimum support prices for the agri-products but also due to availability of alternative employment opportunities.

In 2008, the rural areas grew at a robust rate of 25% as compared to 10% growth in urban retail market. Rural India would become bigger than the total consumer market in countries such as South Korea or Canada in another twenty years. While the per capita income is lower than urban areas, the customer base is thrice that of urban areas.

Resilient to Slowdown

On account of negligible tax liability and little or no burden of loan repayments, the Indian rural population has a higher propensity to save. The rural areas account for 33% India's total savings. Being more conservative than their urban counterparts, the rural population has not burnt their fingers in the real estate or stock market bust. While 18% of rural India has earnings in the range Rs 45,000 to Rs 215,000 per annum, 58% of urban population earns in this range. However, 27 m individuals form a part of this income bracket in rural areas while in urban areas it is about 29 m; of which large base is already tapped.

No of households (m)

Demographic classification	Urban	Rural	Total
Rich (income greater than Rs. 1 m per annum)	4.8	1.3	6.1
Well off (income greater than Rs. 0.5 m per annum)	29.5	27.4	56.9
Total	34.3	28.7	63.0
% of total	54.4%	45.6%	

As per the Associated Chambers of Commerce and Industry of India (ASSOCHAM), the rural market is becoming increasingly attractive for *FMCG,* automobiles and organized retail businesses. Rural India accounts for more than 40% consumption in major FMCG categories such as personal care, fabric care, and hot beverages. FMCG sector in rural areas is expected to grow by 40% as against 25% in urban areas in the coming quarters. Even auto companies in recent times are witnessing shift in trend as they are gearing to explore the huge market potential lying in the rural areas.

% of households owning products (2008)

	Top 20 cities	Other cities	Rural
Car	23	5	3
Bicycle	37	61	69
Colour TV	68	47	17
AC	5	3	0
Refrigerator	63	34	8
Computer	8	3	1

As rural India becomes more lucrative and the government becomes more committed to its development, schemes like the rural employment guarantee, Bharat Nirman, focus on rural education, debt waiver plan and higher support prices will aid the rural demand. Although the penetration levels are still very low, the scope is huge. And India Inc. is not letting go of this opportunity.

Strategies for Rural Marketing

Rural marketing in India is not much developed there are many hindrances in the area of market, product design and positioning, pricing, distribution and promotion. Companies need to understand rural marketing in a broader manner not only to survive and grow in their business, but also a means to the development of the rural economy. One has to have a strategic view of the rural markets so as to know and understand the markets well. In the context of rural marketing one has to understand the manipulation of marketing mix has to be properly understood in terms of product usage. The following are the strategies of rural marketing:

- **Client and location specific promotion:** Increasing specialization in the farming sector has marketers to this strategy. The marketer under this strategy has to design location and carry out farmer specific promotional campaigns.
- **Joint or co-operative promotion** : A personalized approach is required under this strategy of rural marketing. Under this approach there is a greater scope for private sector and farmer organization to get into input supply and especially into retail distribution, as it is a low risk activity.
- **Bundling of inputs** : In order to reap the benefits of, the economies of the scale a rural marketer has to resort to bundling of inputs. 'Bundling of Inputs' is the process by which the marketer would provide a bundle of products to the retailer so that he can meet the requirements of the farmers in one place.
- **Management of demand** : A marketer apart from maintaining good supplies in terms of quality and quantity also has to focus on the demand side of the operations also. Continuous market research should be undertaken to assess the buyer's needs and problems at various levels so that continuous improvements and innovations can be undertaken for a sustainable market performance.
- **Media** : Rural marketing uses both kinds of media i.e. the traditional media as well as the modern media. The traditional media includes drama, folk theatre e.g. tamsaha, nautanki, street plays, folk songs, wall paintings and proverbs. Marketer uses traditional media because it more accessible, personalized, familiar and carries a high potential for change.

- **Ethics in business :** Ethics occupies a special place in rural marketing, and has been at the heart of all the transactions whether cash or kind. In order to make a lasting impact on the rural clients, the firms need to built a trustful relationship and that is possible by no other means but only by ethical conduct.
- **Partnership for sustainabiliry :** Finally there is a need to build partnership with rural clients for a sustainable business relationship and sustainable marketing relationship. There should be a long-term relationship between the firms and farmers for agro business projects, which are risky, long drawn and technical in nature.

Potential Sectors of Rural Market

The world's second largest populated country, India, is the apple of the eye for the world now. The world economies are seeing it as their potential market. Indian markets in urban areas have grown appreciably and are on the verge of saturation, so corporate have started tapping rural markets, since more than 60 per cent of India's population lives in rural areas.

During this global meltdown and fall of exports, if the Fast Moving Consumer Goods (FMCG) sector has been able to show rising quarterly growths, it is because of the Rural Markets and their rising spending power, which have not been affected by this meltdown. Therefore, consumption trends followed by the rural Indian are considered to be the driver of future growth of companies. And this trend of tapping rural markets is visible across all sectors now, be it FMCG, IT, Banking, education etc. For example, today, India is in better state than China because our GDP is less dependent on exports as compared to them. Thus, tapping the rural markets is most important for us to be a self sustaining economy.

- **FMCG** : Rural consumers spend around 13 per cent of their income, the second highest after food (35 per cent), on fast moving consumer goods (FMCG). The FMCG sector saw rural markets post 20 per cent growth, ahead of the 17-18 per cent growth from urban India, aided by three years of good monsoon, higher prices of farm produce and farm-loan waiver. Most FMCG companies are now working on increasing their distribution in smaller towns and focusing on marketing and operations programme for semi-urban and rural markets. The retail sector has a huge potential for growth as a study shows that opportunities in rural retail sector were estimated to be over $34 billion in the year 2007, which is expected to touch $43 billion by the year 2010. It can be seen from the market that companies like Reliance, Godrej, Subhiksha are expanding in the rural market.
- **Insurance sector** : Insurance sector has one of the biggest potential in the upcoming scenario and the fact lies in the statement that only eight to 10 per cent of the rural households are covered by life insurance. Rural investments are limited to their available option—post offices and a few limited commercial banks rural extension counters. The remaining 90 per cent offer a huge potential as such for the insurance companies. The rural market is vibrant and holds tremendous potential for growth of insurance business, particularly because of the strong saving habits. LIC has a target of selling four million policies in the current financial year.
- **Telecom sector** : Telecom sector is one of the booming sectors of the economy. There are a large number of mobile subscribers in India and with the next 100 million to come from non-urban areas, many Indian mobile-service providers are targeting the rural market with aggressive tariffs and low cost hand sets. In this regard Reliance Communication has

targeted the rural segment by its 'Grameen programme' for rural subscribers. Spice Telecom is into the process of launching local market rates for the commodities across Karnataka to connect with rural customers. BSNL plans a $ 125.38 million to be spent on its rural infrastructure.

- **Banking sector :** Just like the FMCG sector, there is tremendous growth potential in the banking sector, because firstly, the rural masses have the habit of saving and spending only when needed. Secondly, their small credit requirements for agriculture, cottage industry and marriages etc. The Reserve Bank of India (RBI), on an all India basis, 59 per cent of the adult population in the country has bank accounts and 41 per cent don't. In rural areas, the coverage of banks is 39 per cent, against 60 per cent in urban areas. Tapping the rural market by banks becomes all the more important. If there is growth in the banking sector, it benefits the other sectors as well. Reasons being, as banks promote savings in the economy, they speed up the capital formation and then become the source of finance of trade and credit for the other industries.

- **Pharmaceutical :** Pharmaceuticals is increasing its focus on the rural market. The company that largely makes active pharmaceutical ingredients plans to increase its sales by 8-9 per cent mainly from rural areas and has allocated US$ 8.26 million to strengthen the sales force for this segment. The rural and tier-II pharma market will account for almost half of the growth till 2015.

- **Automobiles :** For the auto industry, semi-urban and rural markets contribute close to 40 per cent of sales, led by demand for two-wheelers, entry-level cars and tractors. Significantly, car sales grew 8.3 per cent in June 2009, aided by rising demand in semi-urban and rural markets. Mahindra & Mahindra is bullish on the rural and semi-urban markets, with its utility vehicle. Scorpio clocking 60-65 per cent sales from the rural markets as against 20 per cent earlier. TVS Motor also registered around 50 per cent of its sales from the rural and semi-urban markets.

- **Consumer durables** : Many leading consumer durable companies are now increasing their presence in rural India. Recently, LG has set up 45 area offices and 59 rural and remote-area offices. Moreover, it has outlined plans to invest around US$ 40 million towards development of entry-level products targeted at rural markets. Samsung has also rolled out its 'Dream Home' road show which was to visit 48 small towns in 100 days in an effort to increase brand awareness of its products. The company also plans to expand its sales channel by 25-30 per cent in rural India.

With India entering the globalization mode and the rural revolution being governed by rising purchasing power, increased savings, changing consumer habits, there are sure and positive signs that a new dawn of rural India is going to come.

Challenges in Rural Marketing

Our country is endowed with a good degree of ethnic and regional diversity. The development of the nation largely depends upon the development of the rural population. Mahatma Gandhi had once said: *"India's way is not Europe's. India is not Calcutta and Bombay. India lives in her several hundreds of villages".* India is an agro-based economy and the growth of most of the other sectors of economy is driven by rural demand. Urban market is reaching towards the saturation point, thus bringing in and urgent need to focus on rural development. Moreover, more than 70% of India's population lives in villages and constitutions a big market for industry because of increasing disposal incomes and awareness level. Though it is not easy to enter into the rural market and take a sizeable share of the rural market due to the following reasons:

- **Low literacy** : There are not enough opportunities for education in rural areas. The literacy level is as low (36%) when compared to all-India average of 52%.
- **Seasonal demand** : Demand for goods in rural markets depends upon agricultural situation, as agriculture is the main source of income. Agriculture to a large extent depends upon monsoon and, therefore, the demand or buying capacity is not stable or regular.
- **Transportation** : Many rural areas are not connected by rail transport. Kacha roads become unserviceable during the monsoon and interior villages get isolated.
- **Distribution** : An effective distribution system requires village-level shopkeeper, Mandal/Taluka-level wholesaler or preferred dealer, distributor or stockiest at district level and company-owned depot or consignment distribution at state level. The presence of too many tiers in the distribution system increases the cost of distribution.
- **Communication problems** : Facilities such as telephone, fax and telegram are rather poor in rural areas.
- **Traditional life** : Life in rural areas is still governed by customs and traditions and people do not easily adapt new practices. For example, even rich and educated class of farmers does not wear jeans or branded shoes.
- **Buying decisions** : Rural consumers are cautious in buying and decisions are slow and delayed. They like to give a trial and only after being personally satisfied, do they buy the product.

- **Media for promotions :** Television has made a great impact and large audience has been exposed to this medium. Radio reaches large population in rural areas at a relatively low cost. However, reach of formal media is low in rural households; therefore, the market has to undertake specific sales promotion activities in rural areas like participating in melas or fairs.
- **Cultural factors :** Culture is a system of shared values, beliefs and perceptions that influence the behaviour of consumers. There are different groups based on religion, caste, occupation, income, age, education and politics and each group exerts influence on the behaviour of people in villages.

Conclusion

Rural market has its own set of challenges. Rural market has a tremendous potential that is yet to be tapped. A small increase in rural income, results in an exponential increase in buying power. Therefore, organizations need to unlearn and then relearn the marketing tactics that will enable harnessing the immense rural potential. Thus, future development of India and the growth of India lie in financial inclusion, by tapping the rural markets. This will not only help corporate in fulfilling their social responsibilities, but is important for fueling growth in other industries and to keep the economy growing and moving. Truly, there are fortunes at the bottom of the pyramid.

Rural market witnesses a high demand. It's the rural segment of market that contributes more profit than its urban counterpart. Rural marketing broadly involves reaching customers, understanding their wants, supply of goods and services, and ultimately satisfying consumers, leading to more sales. The general impression is that only agricultural inputs like seeds, fertilizers, pesticides, cattle feed and agricultural machinery has a potential for growth in the rural market. However, there is a growing market for consumer goods now. It has been estimated the rural market is growing at the rate of five times its urban counterpart.

REFERENCES

- *Indian Journal of Marketing* September 2009, Volume-XXXIX.
- K.L.K. Rao and Ramesh Tagat: Rural Marketing—A Developmental Approach.
- Monish Bali, "The Rural Market Likes it Strong", *The Economic Times,* August 23, 2000.
- Neeraj Jha, "Gung-ho on Rural Marketing", *The Financial Express,* June 19, 2000.
- T. P. Gopal Swamy, *"Rural Marketing, Environment"*—Problems and Strategies, Wheeler Publishing, 1997.

WEBSITES

- www.indiainfoline.com
- www.scholargoogle.com
- www.ezinearticles.com
- www.wikipedia.com

CHAPTER

5

Effect of Advertisement Copy on Consumers

Prof. Basant Mehta
Dr. Anurag Mehta

INTRODUCTION

All marketing activities are customer oriented. Everyone today understand that business can smoothly run and earn profit only by providing quality product and after sale service to the customers. With the mass production and intensified competition it has become increasingly difficult to contact, inform, stimulate and satisfy customers. For this task marketers resort to advertising. But to advertise is not so easy, it requires lot of knowledge and skill to develop and present an effective ad Pcopy.

Ad copy includes all elements of advertising message and its presentation, either printed or broadcasted. In this broad sense ad copy for a newspaper includes headlines, subheads, picture captions, slogans, body of copy, pictures, all other reading matter, trademarks, borders, illustrations and visual symbols. Copy for a TV commercial include words to be spoken by the characters in the script, music, sound effects, illustrative material, action and camera cues. An ad copy is the product of collective efforts of copywriters, artists and layout men.

Effective copy maker conceive, develop, prepare and present the ad message in a workable and convincing way so that desired objectives are achieved and ad gives fruitful results. If the ad copy is weak, it will not be able to attract and stimulate the prospects and the ad will turn into a complete, fiasco. So it is utmost important for the advertiser to use effective ad copy. To know which are the effective ad copies that command more viewership and liking and increase sale, the research work is taken into hands.

Components of Ad Copy

There are different parts or segments or components of an ad copy. Generally the ad copy contain the below mentioned components, but in few cases the ad copy may not have any one or more component.

(1) Headline, (2) Sub Headline, (3) Slogan, (4) Illustration, (5) Body of Copy, (6) Closing Idea and (7) Identification Marks.

Kinds/Type of Ad Copy

Generally the ads of different products published in newspapers and magazines and broadcasted on television have great difference in their contents and style of presentation. These ads do not attract or influence us equally. Their designing, pattern, size etc. are different. Actually the advertisers are using differenl advertising messages and appeals. They are depicting or showing the ad in different types. With the increasing modernisation and competition advertisers really developed following kinds/types of ad copies:

(1) Straight Selling Copy, (2) Suggestive Copy, (3) Expository Copy, (4) Descriptive Copy, (5) Competitive Copy, (6) Scientific Copy, (7) Educational Copy, (8) Questioning Copy, (9) Order Copy, (10) Colloquial Copy, (11) Poetic Copy, (12) Institutional Copy, (13) Personality Copy, (14) Humorous Copy, (15) Emotional copy, (16) Testimonial Copy, (17) Exaggeration Copy, (18) Demonstrative Copy, (19) Promotional Copy, (20) Occasional Copy, (21) Illustrative Copy, (22) Elegance Copy, (23) Unique Selling Proposition

(USP) Copy, (24) Drama or Story Copy, (25) Child Innocent Copy, (26) Animated Copy, (27) Mixed Copy, (28) Full and Original Copy, (29) Truncated and Reminder Copy, (30) Tele-Based Copy and (31) Serial Advertising Copy.

As the research is related with the effect of ad copy on consumers of Rajasthan it was considered most appropriate to collect the information directly from the consumers of Udaipur district. To study the effect of various types of ad copy, hundred respondents are selected on random basis. Their views regarding the ads of consumer durables namely TV, washing machine, motorcycle and mobile phone are collected through the systematically designed schedule. As far as consumer non-durables are concerned, facts and data relating to the ads of several brands of tea, hair oil, detergent powder and suiting-shirting are collected from the respondents. The main findings of the study are given below:

I. Comparative Effectiveness of Media

In this research effectiveness of different ad copies relating to consumer durables and non-durables presented through three media channels namely newspaper, magazine and TV are studied.

As we know all these three media are very widely used for advertising. They all influence viewers and contribute into sale but their effectiveness are widely different, it is discussed in table 1.

As far as the influence of ads on sale of consumer products are concerned newspaper ads are almost 3.4 times influencive than magazine ads. TV ads are 5.5 times influencive than magazine ads and 1.6 times influcncive than newspaper ads. There is an exception in case of consumer durables where newspaper ads are as influencive as TV ads in fact they are 9.13% more influencive than TV ads. As far as consumer non-durables are concerned TV ads influence 3.2 times than the newspaper ads. It is very clear that TV is much more effective than newspaper to advertise products and magazine is far lesser effective than newspaper.

Table 5.1. Comparative Effectiveness of Media

S. No.	Type of advertised Product	Persons influenced by newspaper ads	Persons influenced by magazine ads	Persons influenced by TV ads
1.	Tea, Hair Oil, Detergent Powder & Suiting-Shirting	65	36	239
2.	Other consumer non-durables	42	20	104
3.	All consumer non-durables (1+2)	107	56	343
4.	Mobile, Motorcycle, Washing Machine & TV	187	37	180
5.	Oilier consumer durables	52	9	39
6.	All consumer durables (4+5)	239	46	219
7.	All consumer products (3+6)	340	102	562

The same thing is confirmed by the table 5.2 where respondents

Table 5.2. Comparative Ranking Media

Rank	Newspaper			Magazine			TV		
	Weight	Number of persons i.e. Frequency	Points	Weight	Number of persons i.e. Frequency	Points	Weight	Number of persons i.e. Frequency	Points
1	3	29	87	3	3	9	3	68	204
2	2	49	98	2	21	42	2	30	60
3	1	22	22	1	76	76	1	2	2
			207			**127**			**266**

68 respondents ranked TV as number one while 76 respondents ranked magazine as number three. 49

respondents ranked newspaper as number two. In conclusion with maximum points TV is far ahead of newspaper and magazine. While newspaper stands at second position as far as the effectiveness of these three media are concerned.

II. Importance of Ads

Those ads which are effectively presented and able to find place in the memories of respondents are making solid contributions in their product's sale. Heavy contribution of ads into sale of advertised products reflects the importance of advertising. This contribution will increase by around 5% in almost all consumer products (see table 5.3).

Table 5.3. Contribution of ad into sale of advertised product.

(percentage)

	Newspaper		Magazine		Television	
	Ads of selected non-durabies	Ads of selected durables	Ads of selected non-durabies	Ads of selected durables	Ads of selected non-durabies	Ads of selected durables
At Present	72.22	82.74	47.37	25.52	84.75	83.33
In Future	74.74	86.97	50	28.57	88.44	87.90
Growth	3.49	5.11	5.55	11.95	4.35	5.48

Here selected non-durables = Tea, Hair Oil, Detergent Powder and Suiting-Shirting.
Here selected durables = Mobile, Motorcycle, Washing Machine & TV.

III. Growth of Advertising Effectiveness

The influence of ads on respondents to use the product will increase in all consumer durables & non-durables. Growth of around 10% can be seen in consumer non-durables, while growth of around 20% can be seen in consumer durables with an exception of nearly 30% growth in the users influenced by magazine ads of consumer durables. In conclusion advertising effectiveness will grow at good pace so it is handy to advertise more. The details are given in table 5.4.

Table 5.4. Growth of advertising effectiveness

	Newspaper		Magazine		Television	
	Ads of selected non-durabies	Ads of selected durables	Ads of selected non-durabies	Ads of selected durables	Ads of selected non-durabies	Ads of selected durables
At Present	65	187	36	37	239	180
In Future	71	227	40	48	260	218
Growth	9.23%	21.39%	11.11%	29.73%	8.79%	19.44%

Here selected non-durables = Tea, Hair Oil, Detergent Powder & Suiting-Shirting and selected durables = Mobile, Motorcycle; Washing Machine & TV

IV. Ads Which are Liked are More Effective

Translation of liking into sale is far ahead of translation of sheer watching into sale. Ads which are more liked are more useful and effective. The chances of their translation into sale are considerably very high. If an attempt is made to formulate a single rule applicable to all the media channels and consumer durables as well as non-durables by summing up the data, it will give misleading and inappropriate results because the higher effectiveness of translation of liking into sale differs widely from product to product and media to media ranging from 40% to 300%. But it is certain that if the effective ad copies, recommended hereinafter for every product and media category is made, it will be more liked and will influence more prospects.

V. Size of Ads

(*i*) In newspaper : 44% respondents suggested that the ad should be of less than quarter page, 35% said it should be quarter page, 12% said it should be half page and 9% suggested that it should be of full page.

Newspaper is read just once and that too in a hurry so the readers don't have time to read big and lengthy ads. People read newspapers not for ads but for the news and informations so they just turn over or switch to the next page as soon as (hey see full page eovered with ad. Hence it is wise to place the ads among news and that is only possible when the size of ad is short. Very short ads even go unnoticed so they should be reasonably short or quarter page.

***(ii)* In magazine :** 31% respondents suggested that the ad should be of full page, 27% said it should be half page, 24% said it should be quarter page and 18% suggested that it should be of less than quarter page.

Magazines are generally read in leisure so the readers may give enough time and attention to the bigger ads and care fully read the whole ad. Bigger ads are more catchy and attractive. Even when a magazine is read again, a cursory look of a big illustrative ad can make a memorable picture in the mind of reader.

***(iii)* On TV :** 68% respondents suggested that ad should be short, 24% said it should be very short, 8% suggested that it should be long and no one suggested very long ad.

Generally entertainment programmes are seen on TV so the viewers do not like ad of long duration, they want the ad to be completed shortly. Today multi channel facility is available, if long ad is broadcasted viewer will quickly switch to some other channel and start watching something else. The same thing will happen if several ads are broadcasted in a row. Besides that if the ad is too short it won't be able to convey the advertising message convincingly so the ad should be reasonably short.

The table 5.5 reveals there was none who could not recognize any slogan or pharase. This is a significant indication showing the popularity of slogans which can be handy for popularizing the product. 47% respondents recognize 5 to 8 slogans out of 32 stated slogans. It implies slogans find place in the memories of prospectus so it is effective to advertise using slogans.

VI. The Memorability of Slogans

Table 5.5. Memorability of Slogans

S.No.	Number of Slogans/ Pharases	Persons who rightly associated the product name
1.	1-4	38
2.	5-8	47
3.	9-12	9
4.	13-16	5
5.	17-20	1
6.	21 & above	—
		100

VII. Ad Copies Effective for Consumer Non-durables

Comparative effectiveness of each ad copy is judged by the influence it make on the viewers to buy the advertised product. In this process equal weight is given to both, the selected products (tea, hair oil, detergent powder and suiting-shirting) and all other non-durable products.

(*i*) **In newspaper** : Illustrative, straight selling, USP, promotional and personality copies are effective as they influence 37.06%, 24.75%, 13.54%, 7.62% & 7.33% of all influenced users respectively.

(*ii*) **In magazine** : Illustrative, USP, personality and descriptive copies are effective as they influence 37.78%, 19.18%, 18.80% & 11.08% of all influenced users respectively.

(*iii*) **On TV** : USP, drama, poetic and personality copies are effective as they influence 26.69%, 25.52%, 16.75% and 14.51% of all influenced users respectively.

(A) Ad Copies Effective for Tea

(*i*) **In newspaper** : Illustrative, promotional, personality and straight selling copies are effective as they influence 39.13%, 26.09%, 21.74% & 13.04% of all influenced users respectively.

(*ii*) **In magazine :** Illustrative, personality and promotional copy are effective as they influence 55.56%, 33.33% & 11.11% of all influenced users respectively.

(*iii*) **On TV :** Drama, USP, personality and poetic copy are effective as they influence 32.28%, 30.71%, 22.84% & 7.87% of all influenced users respectively.

(B) Ad Copies Effective for Hair Oil

(*i*) **In newspaper :** Illustrative, USP, personality and descriptive copies are effective as they influence 33.33%, 33.33%, 16.07% & 16.67% of all influenced users respectively.

(*ii*) **In magazine :** Personally, USP and illustrative copies are effective as they influence 41.93%, 25.81% and 19.35% of all influenced users respectively.

(*iii*) **On TV :** USP, drama, personality and poetic copies are effective as they influence 41.24%, 20.62%, 19.59% & 18.55% of all innucnced users respectively.

(C) Ad Copies Effective for Detergent Powder

(*i*) **In newspaper :** Illustrative, straight selling, USP, and truncated copies are effective as they influence 26.32%, 26.32%, 23.68% & 23.68%) of all influenced users respectively.

(*ii*) **In magazine :** Illuslrntivc, straight selling and USP copies are effective as they influence 46.67%, 33.33% & 20% of all influenced users respectively.

(*iii*) **On TV :** Drama, poetic, USP and child innocent copies are effective as they influence 38.89%, 23.45%, 19.14% & 11.11% of all influenced users respectively.

(D) Ad Copies Effective for Suiting-Shirting

(*i*) **In newspaper :** Only straight selling and illustrative copies are remembered by the respondents and they are equally effective.

(*ii*) **In magazine :** Only illustrative copy is remembered by the respondents and it is quite effective.

(*iii*) **On TV** : Elegance, poetic, USP, personality and drama copies are effective as they influence 25.58%, 24.42%, 20.93%, 16.28% & 10.47% of all influenced users respectively.

VIII. Ad Copies of Effectiveness for Consumer Durables

Comparative effectiveness of each ad copy is judged by the influence it make on the viewers to buy the advertised product. In this process equal weight is given to both, the selected products (mobile, motorcycle, washing machine and TV) and all other durable products.

(*i*) **In newspaper** : Promotional, descriptive, illustrative, USP and personality copies are effective as they influence 33.10%, 24.70%, 19.35%, 11.58% & 10.07% of all influenced users respectively.

(*ii*) **In magazine** : Illustrative, descriptive and USP copies are effective as they influence 43.90%, 31.40% & 18.38% of all influenced users respectively.

(*iii*) **On TV** : USP, poetic, personality and drama copies are effective as they influence 32.43%, 21.83%, 14.31% & 13.99% of all influenced users respectively.

(A) Ad Copies Effective for Mobile Phone

(*i*) **In newspaper** : Descriptive, promotional and USP copies are effective as they influence 47.92%, 32.29%, & 9.37% of all influenced users respectively.

(*ii*) **In magazine** : Illustrative, promotional and descriptive copies are effective as they influence 34.89%, 30.23% & 30.23% of all influenced users respectively.

(*iii*) **On TV** : USP and poetic copies are effective as they influence 50.96% & 41.34% of all influenced users respectively.

(B) Ad Copies Effective for Motorcycle

(*i*) **In newspaper** : Promotional, illustrative, descriptive and USP copies are effective as they influence 34.68%, 22.58%, 18.55% & 13.71% of all influenced users respectively.

(*ii*) **In magazine :** Only illustrative, USP and descriptive copies are remembered by respondents and they are equally effective.

(*iii*) **On TV :** Poetic, drama, USP, exaggeration and personality copies are effective as they influence 33.33%, 20.90%, 20.90%, 13.16% & 9.65% of all influenced users respectively.

(C) Ad Copies Effective for Washing Machine

(*i*) **In newspaper :** Promotional, descriptive, USP and illustrative copies are effective as they, influence 37.68%, 23.19%, 20.29% & 17.39% of all influenced users respectively.

(*ii*) **In magazine :** Illustrative, descriptive and USP copies are effective as they influence 41.18%, 41.18% & 17.64% of all influenced users respectively.

(*iii*) **On TV :** USP, personality, poetic, demonstrative, drama and humorous copies are effective as they influence 33.33%, 17.46%, 14.29%, 14.29%, 11.11%, & 9.52% of all influenced users respectively.

(D) Ad Copies Effective for TV Sets

(*i*) **In newspaper :** Promotional, illustrative, descriptive and personality copies are effective as they influence 29.35%, 27.17%, 21.74% & 18.48% of all influenced users respectively.

(*ii*) **In magazine :** Only illustrative, USP and descriptive copies are remembered by the respondents and they are equally effective.

(*iii*) **On TV :** USP, personality and elegance copies are effective as they influence 33.33%, 33.33% & 28% of all influenced users respectively.

Note: All influenced users here implies the users who are influenced by the ads of a particular product category published or broadcasted in a particular media.

Table 5.6. Comparative Ranking of Ad Copies.

Rank	Drama			Poetic			Personality			Descriptive			Emotional		
	A	B	C	A	B	C	A	B	C	A	B	C	A	B	C
1	11	19	209	11	17	187	11	16	176	11	13	143	11	9	99
2	10	16	160	10	21	210	10	14	140	10	15	150	10	15	150
3	9	18	162	9	10	90	9	9	81	9	15	135	9	7	63
4	8	15	120	8	9	72	8	13	104	8	14	112	8	6	48
5	7	12	84	7	13	91	7	7	49	7	8	56	7	17	119
6	6	5	30	6	5	30	6	14	84	6	2	12	6	6	36
7	5	7	35	5	11	5	5	2	10	5	8	40	5	12	60
8	4	3	12	4	2	8	4	15	60	4	7	28	4	10	40
9	3	1	3	3	5	15	3	10	30	3	9	27	3	14	42
10	2	2	4	2	3	6	2	—	0	2	3	6	6	2	3
11	1	2	2	1	4	4	1	—	0	1	6	6	1	1	1
			821			768			734			715			664

Table 5.6. (Contd.)

Rank	Humorous			Competitive			Scientific			Testimonial			Colloquial			Questioning		
	A	B	C	A	B	C	A	B	C	A	B	C	A	B	C	A	B	C
1	11	7	77	11	6	66	11	8	88	11	5	55	11	—	0	11	—	0
2	10	8	80	10	5	50	10	4	40	10	2	20	10	—	0	10	—	0
3	9	17	153	9	12	108	9	8	72	9	4	36	9	—	0	9	—	0
4	8	12	96	8	9	72	8	9	72	8	1	8	8	7	56	8	5	40
5	7	9	63	7	13	91	7	10	70	7	—	0	7	8	56	7	3	21
6	6	12	72	6	15	90	6	7	42	6	14	84	6	11	66	6	9	54
7	5	7	35	5	15	75	5	16	80	5	8	40	5	3	15	5	11	55
8	4	11	44	4	7	28	4	15	60	4	26	104	4	4	16	4	—	0
9	3	3	9	3	4	12	3	8	24	3	15	45	3	16	48	3	15	45
10	2	5	10	2	6	12	2	12	24	2	19	38	2	22	44	2	25	50
11	1	9	9	1	8	8	1	3	3	1	6	6	1	29	29	1	32	32
			648			**612**			**575**			**436**			**330**			**297**

(IX) Comparative Ranking of Ad Copies

An effort is made to judge the comparative effectiveness of ad copies in general, without considering any specific media or product. For that purpose eleven ad copies which were popular and considered effective prior to the study, were mentioned in the schedule to be ranked on the basis of their effectiveness.

Respondents give different rank to these ad copies. To draw a clear and categorical conclusion the table 5.6 is prepared. Higher weights are assigned to the higher ranks and lower weights are assigned to the lower ranks. Table shows with higher points drama, poetic, personality and descriptive copies stand 1st, 2nd, 3rd and 4th respectively. Other research findings stated previously also confirms that drama, poetic and personality copies are effective for advertising consumer non-durables and durables on TV, though it tells USP copy is the most effective. It also confirms that personality and descriptive copies are effective for advertising in newspaper and magazine.

Emotional, humorous and competitive copies stands 5th, 6th and 7th respectively that implies they are reasonably effective. Scientific, testimonial, colloquial and questioning copies are ranked very low by most of the respondents so they stand 8th, 9th, 10th and 11th respectively. They are very little effective.

(X) Ads which are not Good

(*i*) **In newspaper** : Only 7% respondents mention the name of just few products whose ad they do not consider good. When these ads are analysed it is found that they are lacking bclievability and are almost unbelievable.

(*ii*) **In magazine** : It is astonishing that no one really dislike the ads published in magazine as not a single respondent mentioned the name of product whose ad they consider not good or bad.

(*iii*) **On TV** : Merely 8% respondents mention the name of just few products whose ad they do not consider good. These ads use too long and descriptive copy. When respondents were asked about the size they also preferred short ad copies. Product categorywise research findings also reveal that descriptive copy is not. suitable for TV. TV is seen for entertainment and descriptive copy cause boredom. The personality choosen is not suitable for or not relevant to the product. These ads were also lacking believability.

In general respondents do not really dislike the ads that are presented today. It can be concluded that ads made today are of good taste, they do not offend or instigate the viewers in any way, they are not violating the social norms and following the code of conduct.

Test of Research Hypotheses

1. **"The influence of different ad copy on consumers is not similar'** : As far as ads of mobile published in newspaper are concerned descriptive, promotional, USP, personality and illustralive copies influence 47.92%, 32.29%, 9.37%, 6.25% & 4.17% of all influenced viewers.

As far as ads of tea broadcasted on TV are concerned drama, USP, personality, poetic, elegance, exaggeration and promotional copies influence 32.28%, 30.71%, 22.84%, 7.87%, 4.72%, 0.79% & 0.79% of all influenced viewers. Similarly with other products we can easily find big difference in the influence of different ad copies.

Hence the hypothesis "The influence of different ad copy on consumers is not similar" is accepted

2. **"Same type of ad copy cannot he useful for print and for television media"** : In newspaper and magazine illustrative copy is the best to advertise consumer non-durables ad its share in all influenced viewers is 37.06% & 37.78% respectively. While in case of tele media illustrative

copy stands nowhere, it is not at all effective. Similarly descriptive copy is very effective to advertise consumer durables in newspaper and magazine as its share in all influenced viewers is 24.70% & 31.40% respectively. While on TV descriptive copy is not at all effective.

Poetic copy is very effective to advertise on TV ad its share in all influenced viewers is 16.75% in case of non-durables and 21.83% in case of durables. While Poetic copy is not at all effective for advertising in newspaper and magazine.

It all implies that same type of ad copy cannot be useful for print and for tele media.

Personality copy is effective for advertising consumer non-durables in all three media channels. Its share in the total influenced viewers is 7.33% in newspaper, 18.80% in magazine and 14.51% in TV. Similarly USP copy is also effective for advertising consumer durables and non-durables in all three media channels. Though it is best on TV but just reasonably good in newspapers and magazines. So the same ad copy can be effective for print and tele media. Though the influence may vary from media to media.

In conclusion same type of ad copy may or may not be useful for both the print and television media. Hence the hypothesis is partially accepted.

3. "For consumer durables scientific ad copy and for consumer non-durables competitive ad copy are most effective" : For consumer durables promotional copy is best in newspaper, illustrative copy is best in magazine and USP copy is best on TV.

For consumer non-durables illustrative copy is best in newspaper and magazine, while USP copy is the best on TV.

Not a single respondent mentioned any durable product that uses scientific copy or any non-durable product that uses competitive copy, in any of the three media channel. Hence the hypothesis is rejected and it is concluded that scientific and competitive ad copies are absolutely ineffective.

Recommendations

1. Ads are making huge contributions in the sale of advertised product and it will increase in future so it is advised to use ads regularly to keep the product live in the memories of prospects and increase sale.
2. TV is the best media channel so it is adviseable to use it for advertising the products specially for non-durable products. TV is far better than newspaper and magazine.
3. For advertising durable products both the TV and newspaper are almost equally effective so both media channels should be used.
4. 68% respondents preferred short ads so short ad copy should be prepared for TV and that too should be broadcasted where commercial breaks are not of long duration.
5. Less than quarter page ads and quarter page ads are preferred by 44% & 35% respondents respectively. Hence reasonably short or quarter size ads should be prepared and placed among news, it should not be surround by several other ads.
6. Full page ads and half page ads are preferred by 31% & 27% respondents respectively so as far as budget permits bigger ads should be prepared for advertising in magazine.
7. Believable facts, claims and information should be given in the ad and the presentation should also be believable.
8. Slogans easily find place in the memories of prospects so they should be included and prominently shown or emphasized in the ad copy.

9. Ads made today are of good taste and respondents like them. The ads are decent and following the social norms and ideal code of conduct so any additional law or external check is not required to be imposed on ads.
10. Illustrative, straight-selling and USP copy influence 37.06%, 24.75% & 13.54% of all influenced users respectively. Considering their higher effectiveness illustrative, straight selling and USP copies are recommended to advertise consumer non-durables in newspaper.
11. Illustrative, USP, personality and descriptive copy influence 37.78%, 19.18%, 18.80% & 11.08% of all influenced users respectively. Considering their higher effectiveness illustrative, USP, personality and descriptive copies are recommended to advertise consumer non-durables in magazine.
12. USP, drama, poetic and personality copy influence 26.69%, 25.52%, 16.75% & 14.51% of all influenced users respectively. Considering their higher effectiveness USP, drama, poetic and personality copies are recommended to advertise consumer non-durables on TV.
13. Promotional, descriptive, illustrative, USP and personality copy influence 33.10%, 24.70%, 19.35%, 11.58% & 10.07%, of all influenced users respectively. Considering their higher effectiveness promotional, descriptive, illustrative, USP and personality copies are recommended to advertise consumer durables in newspaper.
14. Illustrative, descriptive and USP copy influenced 43.90% 31.40% & 18.38% of influenced users respectively. Considering their higher effectiveness illustrative, descriptive and USP copies are recommended to advertise consumer durables in magazine.
15. USP, poetic, personality and drama copy influence 32.43%, 21.83%, 14.31% & 13.99%, of all influenced

users respectively. Considering their higher effectiveness USP, poetic, personality and drama copies are recommended to advertise consumer durables on TV.

REFERENCES

Books

Antebi, Michael	The Art of Creative Advertising, Reimhold Book Corporation, New York, 1968.
Burton R. Durkee	How to make Advertising Work, McGraw Hill Book Co., New York, 1967.
Caple John	Making Advertisements Pay, Harper & Row Publishers Incorporated, New York, 1957.
Divita S.F.	Advertising and the Public Interest, American Marketing Association, Chicago, 1975.
David W. Stward & David F. Furse	Effective TV Advertising : A Study of 1000 Commercials, MA Lexington Books, Lexington, 1986.
Heighten, Elizabeth J. & Don R. Cunningham	Advertising in Broadcast Media, Wadsworth Publishing Co. Inc., Belmont, Calif, 1976.
Higgings Denis	The Art of Writing Advertising, Advertising Publications Inc., Chicago, 1965
Hurwood, David L. & Earl L. Bailey	Advertising, Sales Promotion and Public Relations-Organisational Alternatives, The National Industrial Conference Board, Inc., New York, 1968.
Jacobs, Laurence W.	Advertising and Promotion for Retailing : Text and Cases, Scott, Foresman & Co., Glenview, 1972.
Leo Bogart	Strategy in Advertising, Harcourt Brace Jovanovich, New York, 1967.
Quera Leon	Advertising Campaigns : Formulation and Tactics, Grid Inc., Columbus, Ohio, 1973.
Rathor B.S.	Advertising Management, Himalaya Publishing House, Bombay, 1995.
Sharma Sandeep and Kumar Deepak	Advertising Planning, Implementation and Control, Mangal Deep Publications, Jaipur, 2001.

Singh D.R., Upadhyay K.M, Tandon R.K. and Das N.K. — Advertising with Special Reference to India, Kalyani Publishers, New Delhi, 1981.

Sissors, Jack Z. & E. Reynold Petray — Advertising Media Planning, Crain Books, Chicago, 1976.

Sontakki CN — Advertising, Kalyani Publishers, New Delhi, 1996.

Stridsberg, Albert B. — Effective Advertising Self-Regulation : A Survey of Current World Practice and Analysis of International Patterns, International Advertising Association, New York, 1974.

Wainwright Anthony Charles — The Television Copywriter, Communication Arts Books, Hasting House Publishers Inc., New York, 1966.

Walter Weir — On The Writing of Advertising, McGraw-Hill Book Co., New York, 1960.

Whitter, Charles L. — Creative Advertising, Holt, Rinehart and Winston Inc., New York, 1955.

Wright S. John Warner S. Daniel, Winter L. Wills Jr., Zeigler K. Sherilyn — Advertising, Tata McGraw-Hill Publishing Co. Ltd., 1981.

Young, James Webb — How to Become an Advertising Man, Advertising Publications Inc., Chicago, 1963.

Articles :

Agrawal D.P. — Role of Advertising in Sales Promotion of Drugs in India, Indian Journal of Marketing.

Appel, Valentine & Babette Jockson — Copu Testing in Competitive Environment, Journal of Marketing, Vol. 39.

Armstrong, Gray M. & Frederick A. — Detecting Decemtion in Advertising, MSU Business Topics, Vol. 23.

Baker. Michael J. and Gilbert A. Churchill, Jr. — The Impact of Physically Attrative Models on Advertising Evaluations, Journal of Advertising Research, XIV.

Chance, Paul	Ads Without Answers Make the Brain Itch, Psychology Today.
Nakanishi, Masao	Advertising and Promotional Effect on Consumer Response to New Product, Journal of Marketing Research.
Shukla P.K.	Measuring the Effectiveness of Advertising in North-West Region, MBA Training Report, Dept. of Business Management, PAV Ludhiana.

CHAPTER

6

Marketing Strategies of L.I.C. of India Transformation of Monopoly into a Stiff Competitor

Prof. Rajeev Jain
Dr. Sarita Bhatnagar
Dr. Vikas Bhatnagar

LIC of India—Profile

Since nationalization, Life Insurance business in India is coterminous with the state owned LIC, which has a dominant position in the economy in two ways. First, as a national insurance agency it serves to pool and redistribute risks associated with the death of insurers (policy-holders) in millions of households. In many cases, insurance policies provide for savings for old age. Life insurance is thus important from social point of view. Secondly, as a major collective savings institution, LIC is a dominant financial intermediary in the economy, channelizing the investible funds to the productive sectors. Thus, insurance provides means to mobilize household savings on a large scale for rapid industrialization and self-reliance in heavy industries for the development of the country and also conducting the business in the spirit of trusteeship and providing protection to the people in every part of the country.

The Life Insurance Corporation of India was set-up by the Government of India to achieve the following objectives:

- Spreading Life Insurance much more widely and in particular to the rural areas and to the socially and economically backward classes with a view to reaching all insurable persons in the country and providing them adequate financial cover against death at a reasonable cost.
- Maximizing mobilization of people's savings by making insurance linked savings adequately attractive.
- Deploying the funds to the best advantage of the investors as well as the community as a whole, keeping in view national priorities and obligations of attractive return.
- Conducting business with utmost economy and with the full realization that the moneys belong to the policyholders.
- Acting as trustees of the insured public in their individual and collective capacities.
- Meeting the various life insurance needs of the community that would arise in the changing social and economic environment.
- Involving all people working in the Corporation to the best of their capability in furthering the interests of the insured public by providing efficient service with courtesy.
- Promoting amongst all agents and employees of the Corporation a sense of participation, pride and job satisfaction through discharge of their duties with dedication towards achievement of Corporate Objective.

LIC has been a beneficial provider of Finance to national projects and an imaginative investment of social welfare. Life Insurance Corporation of India (LIC) is a multi-division, multi-branch organisation which has its presence in every nook and corner of the country. It has 7 zonal offices, 100 Divisional offices and 2048 branch offices with an agent's strength of 1028904 as on March 31, 2005. The corporation also maintains its presence in Fiji, Mauritius and United Kingdom.

Over a period of time LIC has come out with a number of policies for different sections of society which aim at specific objectives. The notable ones are: Varistha Pension Bima Yojna, New Jeevan Shree-I, Jeevan Saral, Bima Nivesh 2004, etc.

Important Activities

The important activities with which the premier life assurance company is associated are as follows:

1. Creating an awareness among the masses about the importance of life assurance and spreading the message of insurance.
2. Acting as a trustee by condition business with maximum economy.
3. Adopting practices and selling products according to the changing need of the people.
4. Maximising the mobilisation of savings and providing funds for the development of the country.
5. Involving all people of the corporation in an effort to provide the best services to the customer by giving efficient services "with a smile".
6. Diversifying the additional resources through Housing Loan and Mutual Fund to generate further funds. To make all these activities successful, LIC has more than 50 products range catering to the various needs such as pay back policies, health related, children-benefits, women, old age pension, mentally and physically threatened people and so on. To take care, of all these products and provide efficient services, the LIC has:

(*a*) Management Development Centre at Mumbai,

(*b*) Zonal Training Centres,

(*c*) Sales Training Centres, and

(*d*) Agent Training Centres.

Organisational Set-up

The LIC has its Central Office in Mumbai with zonal offices at Mumbai, Kolkata, Chennai, Delhi, Hyderabad, Bhopal and Kanpur. In addition to these it has 100 divisional offices and 2048 branch offices each having specific functions and powers. Also these offices have their own geographical boundaries of operations clearly demarcated. As a matter of fact most of the business is conducted through the branch offices which account for 90% of the business transactions mainly related to the policy holders. However, any investment in whatsoever means, is done through the central office at Mumbai. The division of zones is in tandem with the business and the zonal office controls the divisional offices and similarly the branch offices are monitored by the divisional office.

The organisational hierarchy is proceeded by a Chairman, appointed by the Government of India, to whom two Managing Directors report and they are in turn reported by the Executive Directors. The different Zonal Managers report to the Executive Directors. The remaining hierarchy is as follows, starting from the lowest till the Zonal Managers.

Assistants : Higher Grade Assistants—Assistant Administrative Officers—Administrative Officers—Assistant Divisional Managers—Divisional Managers—Senior Divisional Managers—Zonal Managers.

Beside the set-up in India, LIC has foreign offices located at London, Mauritius and Fiji controlled by the Central Office. In addition LIC also has LIC Mutual Fund and LIC Housing Finance Ltd.

Product Offered by LIC of India

Product offered by LIC of India is shown in Table No. 6.1.

Table 6.1. Products Offered by LIC of India

(I) Insurance Plans

(A) Children's Plan

1. Jeevan Anurag
2. CDA Endowment Vesting at 21
3. CDA Endowment Vesting at 18
4. Jeevan Kishore
5. Child Career Plan
6. Child Fortune Plus
7. Komal Jeevan
8. Marriage Endowment Educational Annuity Plan
9. Jeevan Chhaya
10. Child Future Plan

(B) Plans for Handicapped Dependents

1. Jeevan Aadhar
2. Jeevan Vishwas

(C) Endowment Assurance Plans

1. The Endowment Assurance Policy
2. The Endowment Assurance Policy Limited Payment
3. Jeevan Mitra (Double Cover Endowment Plan)
4. Jeevan Mitra (Triple Cover Endowment Plan)
5. Jeevan Anand
6. New Janraksha Plan
7. Jeevan Amrit

(D) Plans for High Worth Individuals

1. Jeevan Shree-1
2. Jeevan Pramukh

(E) Money Back Plans

1. The Money Back Policy (20 years)
2. The Money Back Policy (25 years)
3. Jeevan Surabhi (15 years)
4. Jeevan Surabhi (20 years)

5. Jeevan Surabhi (25 years)
6. Bima Bachat

(F) Special Money Back Plan for Women

1. Jeevan Bharati

(G) Whole Life Plans

1. The Whole Life Policy
2. The Whole Life Policy (Limited Payment)
3. The Whole Life Policy (Single Premium)
4. Jeevan Anand
5. Jeevan Tarang

(H) Term Assurance Plans

1. Two-Year Temporary Assurance Policy
2. The Convertible Term Assurance Policy
3. Anmol Jeevan-1
4. Amulya Jeevan- 1

(I) Joint Life Plan

1. Jeevan Saathi Plus
2. Jeevan Saathi

(J) Pension Plans

1. Jeevan Nidhi
2. Jeevan Akshay-VI
3. New Jeevan Dhara-1
4. New Jeevan Suraksha-1

(K) Unit Plans

1. Market Plus-1
2. Profit Plus
3. Money Plus-1
4. Child Fortune Plus
5. Jeevan Saathi Plus

(L) Special Plans

1. Jeevan Nischay (Single Premium Plan)
2. New Bima Gold

3. Health Protection Plus
4. Health Plus
5. Bima Nivesh (Single Premium- 2005)
6. Jeevan Saral (With Profit)
7. Jeevan Madhur (Micro Insurance)
8. Jeevan Mangal (Micro Insurance)

(M) Group Schemes

1. Group LIC's Superannuation Plus
2. Group Term Insurance Schemes
3. Group Insurance Scheme in Lieu of EDLI
4. Group Gratuity Scheme
5. Group Superannuation Scheme
6. Group Savings Linked Insurance Scheme
7. Group Leave Encashment Scheme
8. Group Mortgage Redemption Assurance Scheme
9. Gratuity Plus
10. Group Critical Illness Rider

(N) Social Security Schemes

1. Jan Shree Bima Yojana (For people below poverty line)
2. Shiksha Sahayog Yojana
3. Aam Aadmi Bima Yojana (Rural Landless Household)

Current Status

LIC mopped-up a premium of Rs. 25,814.49 crore in HI FY 10, registering a growth of 35 per cent, as against Rs. 19,091.48 crore is the corresponding period last year. In year 2008-2009. LIC's first year premium stood at Rs. 529 billion. In the year 2007-08 LIC maintained 61.91 % market share in premium and 73.92% in individual policies. The alternate channel contribution to business is rising steadily with a growth of 51.32% in policies and 21.66% in FPI and percentage share to total new business has gone up from 1.31% to 2.01 % in policies and 1.68% to 1.84% in FPI.

LIC has been conferred "Skoch challenger Award 2008" for Financial Inclusion in Insurance sector through Jeevan Madhur initiatives. During the year 2007-08, LIC completed 375.90 lacs new policies and the total number of inforce policies of LIC crossed the mark of 23 crore individual insurance. LIC is the largest user of information technology in the insurance sector and it has networked all its 2048 tranches and 340 satellite offices to provide the convenience of any time premium payment to all its policy holders.

MARKETING STRATEGIES OF LIC : A COMPARISON OF PRE AND POST LIBERALISED ERA

Till privatization Life Insurance Corporation of India was the only company providing Life Insurance services in India. LIC sold its policies as tax saving instruments and not as products giving protection against risk. Most of the customers were underinsured with no flexibility or transparency in the services provided. Before the entry of private players, insurance penetration and awareness was very low especially in rural India. Most of the plans offered by LIC were highly standardized offering least flexibility and choice to customers. The customer centricity and innovation was not a prominent observation in the way marketing strategies were carried out by LIC premium payment was possible only through branch offices and agents .Information availability regarding various aspects of plans and future service requirements was very less. Professionalisation and agents training was given a very little importance. The only channel of distribution was Agents and no effort was there to innovate into alternate channels of distribution. But after the entry of private Life insurance companies and rapid expansion of their market base as a result of aggressive marketing strategies adopted by them LIC had to reinvent itself as competitor in the market. The rapidly dropping market share forced a new approach towards marketing strategies to be adopted. The paradigm shift in LIC's marketing strategies is discussed as follows:

Table 6.2. The Population and Life Insurance Business from 1980-81 to 2004-05

Year	Premium	Population	Number of Policies
1981	148.79	668.31	1,954,424
1982	158.39	683.30	2,103,134
1983	181.21	698.07	2,231,385
1984	191.25	713.17	2,366,057
1985	225.57	728.58	2,699,654
1986	286.69	744.34	3,285,607
1987	373.49	760.43	3,868,316
1988	531.62	776.87	4,693,788
1989	715.93	793.66	5,979,260
1990	980.98	810.82	7,392,251
1991	1,195.85	828.35	8,645,386
1992	1,405.05	846.26	9,238,264
1993	1,616.58	883.90	9,957,848
1994	1,899.81	899.90	10,725,633
1995	2,055.75	916.00	10,874,682
1996	2,332.13	939.50	11,020,825
1997	2,612.94	955.20	12,268,476
1998	3,195.17	971.00	13,311,294
1999	3,986.60	988.00	14,843,687
2000	4,756.10	1,005.00	16,976,782
2001	5,590.75	1,012.40	19,656,663
2002	6,965.00	1,027.60	22,491,304
2003	8,288.87	1,043.50	24,278,775
2004	10,885.93	1,060.00	27,740,916
2005	11,192.31	1,076.90	31,122,534

Source: CMIE, Annual Report of LIC (various issues).

Table 6.3. LIC—Some Basic Statistics : 1957-2006.

S. No.		As on 31 December 1957	As on 31 March 2000	As on 31 March 2006
1.	Business in Force			
	No. of policies (in lakh)	56.86	1,013.89	1,796.63
	Sum assured (in corre)	14.00	536,450.82	1,282,467.87
	(Individual assurance only)			
2.	Premium Income			
	First year (in crore)	13.72	4,956.10	12,805.56
	Renewal (in crore)	74.35	19,251.88	56,915.71
	Total Premium (in crore)	88.65	27,461.71	90,759.20
3.	Policy Payments			
	Death claim (in crore)	7.89	1,637.70	3,769.04
	Maturity claim (in crore)	20.81	7,628.55	24,743.42
	Total	28.70	9,266.25	28,512.46
4.	(*a*) Life fund (in crores)	410.41	154,043.73	463,147.62
	(*b*) Total assets (in crore)	465.04	161,002.22	552,447.33
5.	Investment (Rs. in crore)	381.90	139,032.15	524,017.25
6.	Government's share (5%) in valuation	14.50	265.02	621.77
7.	Number of divisional offices	33	100	101
8.	Number of branches	240	2,048	2,048
9.	Number of agents on roll	207,373	714,615	1,052.283
10.	Number of employees on roll	30,768	122,867	113,184
11.	Expense ratio	27.30%	21.16%	14.47%

Source : First Statutory Report of LIC (presented to Parliament on 13.3.59 for the first sixteen months from 1.9.56 to 31.12.57) Annual Report of LIC for the year 1999-2000 and 2005-06.

A. Mobilization of Savings

Since nationalization, Indian life insurance industry has registered a significant growth and gradually increased its share in household financial savings. As noted earlier the share of insurance funds in household financial savings has increased from 12.1 per cent in 1999-2000 to 13.0 per cent in 2004-05, while the share of life insurance funds increased from 11.2 per cent to 12.4 per cent during the same period. In terms of GDP it went up from 1.5 per cent to 1.8 per cent. This was a significant achievement of life insurance industry considering the fact that till 2000, the industry was represented by LIC of India alone.

B. Increase in Life Fund and Assets

Growth in Life Fund is considered to be an important indicator of growth of life insurance industry. An organisation which began its journey with a mere asset base of about Rs. 465.04 crore in the first year has successfully accumulated an asset base of Rs. 552,447.33 crore by 31st March 2006, that is, an increase of about 940 times. Similarly, the Life Fund of LIC increased by about 996 times, from Rs. 410.41 crore in 1957 to Rs. 463,147.62 crore in 2006. (Table 6.3) This is an excellent achievement for LIC which sells long-term intangible products like life insurance. This is an excellent achievement particularly in view of the low rate of literacy and lower level of per capita disposable income in India.

C. New Business Growth

High growth of Life Fund and assets of LIC was possible due to significant growth in New Business, which however got a boost during the post-liberalization period. First time in 1999, LIC sold more than one crore (1.48 crore) policies in a single year and in 2006 it crossed the 3 crore mark by selling 3.15 crore policies. During 1999-2000 New Business (Individual Assurance including Annuity) of LIC was Rs 92090.01 crore (SA) under 172.12 lakh policies which increased further to Rs 288,522.55 crore under 31,585,917 policies in 2005-06.

D. Rural Thrust in New Business

LIC is significantly increasing its operations in Rural India, not only in terms of opening up offices, recruiting agents and development officers in rural areas, but rural penetration in terms of New Business. As per the rural/social sector definition of IRDA, New Business from rural areas amounted to Rs. 609,718.5 (SA) under 7,466,484 policies representing 23.65 per cent and 21:21 share of policies and SA, respectively, during the year 2005-06 (LIC Annual Report 2005-06). Similarly, policy payment towards death and maturity claim increased from Rs 28.70 crore in 1957 to Rs 28, 512.46 crore in 2006.

E. Growth Rates—New Business

During 1951-2006, LIC has expanded in many dimensions including New Business, assets and investment. An analysis of growth rate would give us an indication of decadal performance. We may analyze New Business in terms of SA and number of policies. Two outstanding years of achievement in SA growth were 2002 (54.34 per cent) and 1995 (32.08 per cent). The decadal average growth in SA under New Business during 1960-69, 1970-79, 1980-89, 1990-99 and 2000-06 was 8.7 per cent, 8.6 per cent, 24 per cent and 18.5 per cent, respectively, indicating that so far the best decade of growth was 1980s (1980-89) which had average growth of 24 per cent.

The performance of nationalized LIC of India, as assessed in terms of only few areas revealed that LIC has been able to fulfil the expectations of the policymakers, with its outstanding achievement in almost every aspect—providing a Personal Financial Risk Management (PFRM), expanding the life insurance market, spreading insurance in rural areas, promoting savings habit among the people, contributing to national development particularly through socially oriented investment and creating employment opportunities for millions of people in the country. While implementing national planning the Indian government created many national institutions which played a significant role in building today's India and LIC is one such precious institution of India.

F. Premium Income

Increase in life fund and assets was possible due to significant increase in business of LIC. While the first year premium income went up from Rs. 13.72 crore in 1957 to Rs. 12,805.56 crore in 2006, the total premium income increased from Rs. 88.55 crore in 1956 to Rs. 27,461.71 crore in March 2000 and thereafter to 90,759.20 crore in March 2006. Total premium income per employee increased from Rs. 0.288 lakhs in 1956 to Rs. 80.187 lakhs in 2006.

G. In-force Policies

Total number of in-force policies went up from 56.86 lakhs in 1957 to 1,013.89 lakhs in 2000 and thereafter a huge increase to 1,796.63 lakhs in 2006. The number of in-force policies per branch and division was 0.23 lakhs and 1.72 lakhs in 1957 which has gone upto 0.88 lakhs and 17.79 lakhs respectively, for per branch and divisional office.

H. Claims Settlement

During the year 2005-06 LIC has settled a total of 120.90 lakh claims for Rs. 28,512.46 crore. During 2005-06 LIC has settled 115.63 lakhs maturity claims amounting Rs. 24,743.42 crore and 5.27 lakh death claims amounting to Rs. 3,769.04 crore. This has been possible due to massive computerization, networking, thrust on Customer Relationship Management (CRM), etc.

I. Changed Product Profile

Pre Liberalization LIC had been offering only plain policies without any riders. LIC never seemed to have had any proper strategy for bringing out innovative products and customer, friendly pricing of its products. Though the LIC offered around 60 products, only 7 to 8 were popular with the policyholders.

After the entry of private players with innovative products LIC began restructuring its portfolio.

In 2002 'Amulya Jeevan' a new Life Insurance product was launched also in 2002, the LIC offered a new facility-the term insurance rider. Also 'Jeevan Anand' (a combination of an endowment and a whole life plan), 'Jeevan Kekha' (a combination of money back and whole life plan), 'Jeevan Surabhi' (a money back policy) and 'Jeevan Mitra' (an endowment policy) were launched in 2002. In the subsequent years LIC continued to rejig its product portfolio by adding on new plans and riders, with a vision to cover more segments of customers and meet expectations by specific products. Group insurance plans, pensions plans, children plans, health insurance plans, unit-linked plans, micro insurance plans all these diversified and flexible plans were introduced from time to time by LIC to retain the dominant market share.

J. Unit Linked Plans

A major change in product profile of LIC was in terms of introduction of Unit Linked Plans which gain a lot of response because of changing aspiration of customers from Life Insurance Policies. To meet the investment and profit oriented requirement of customers, Unit Linked Plans were offered by LIC. LIC introduced its ULIP "Bima Pans" in 2004 and was successful in pushing it. As of July 2006, LIC registered a growth of 217 per cent in its new business mainly driven by ULIPs.

K. Agents and Employees

There has been a substantial increase in the number of agents on role which has increased by about five times between 1957 (207,373) and 2006 (1,052,283). The corporation has launched an innovative scheme called the

'Urban and Rural Career Agents' with a view to attract educated youth to take up LIC agencies. By March 2005, there were 25,856 urban career agents and 46,418 rural career agents. Thus LIC has directly provided employment opportunity to millions in addition to providing regular employment which has gone up by more than three times from 30,768 in 1957 to 113,184 in 2006.

L. Network of Offices

Office network is an important input for growth in order to reach to the customers for mobilization of business and to take service to the doorsteps of customers. Realizing this LIC moved to build up its office network by opening branch and divisional offices throughout the country. In 1957 LIC started its journey with 33 divisional offices mostly in the metropolitan and urban areas, the number has gone up to 101 and most of these new divisions are in the smaller cities, similarly, the number of branches to start with was 240 in 1957 it increased to 2,048 and most of the new branches are in semi-urban and rural areas. Out of 2,048 branches, 1,248 branch offices of LIC are located in rural areas. Besides 2,048 branches, LIC has opened 24 satellite offices by March 2006 for providing services at the doorstep of the customers. LIC's strategic planning for market penetration takes into account the segmentation and development of rural and urban market. There is a strong network of agents to cater to the needs of rural people.

M. Alternate Channel

LIC significantly raised emphasis an alternative channels and aims to be the leader in business through alternative channels also. LIC has tie-ups with 39 banks across India along with tie-ups with rural banks, cooperative societies, and microfinance institutions. LIC is increasing business through other channels like direct marketing and brokers.

N. Advertising

The ever increasing competition in insurance sector forced LIC to increase its advertising budget. In 2001 LIC brought out "We know India Better" Campaign to attack the private insurers in India. In 1999-2000, prior to privatization LIC had spent Rs. 37 crores on advertising, but as of 2006 LIC had spent Rs. 130 crores in advertising and brand promotion. In order to promote public awareness about the history of LIC, Zindagi Express, an exhibition mounted on a train showcasing the history and achievements of LIC was launched in 2006, LIC's golden jubilee year.

O. Foreign Operation

In the past nationalization period, LIC has not only expanded its offices and marketing network in India but it has also opened several subsidiaries and branch offices.

Branches

LIC has its branch offices at Port Louis (Mauritius), Suva and Laukota (Fiji) and at Wembley (United Kingdom).

Subsidiaries and Joint Venture

LIC (International) BSC (C), Bahrain is a subsidiary of the corporation opened in 1989 which operates in the states of Bahrain, Saudi Arabia, Kuwait and United Arab Emirates (UAE) through chief agents and brokers. This company has opened a branch office in Muscat at Oman. A joint venture is being set up by LIC Saudi Arabia. In Nepal-LIC Nepal Ltd. is functioning as a joint venture between LIC of India and M/s Vishal Group of Companies in the Kingdom of Nepal launched in 2001 and in Sri Lanka LIC has established LIC Lanka Ltd. It is a joint venture company between LIC of India and M/s Bartleet Group of Co. Ltd., launched in 2004. LIC (Mauritius) offshore-a joint venture company between LIC of India and GIC of India.

P. Massive Use of Information Technology

LIC is one of the organizations in India which has gone for massive use of technology. It has its own Software Development Centre (SDC), engaged in upgrading existing technology and developing new technology. In LIC, all the jobs processed in branch offices have been mechanized, 2,042 branches (out of 2,048) are now connected through wide area network, LIC has its own portal providing various services, including policy status, bonus calculation, loan quotation, list of lapsed policies, A similar portal has been in place for the agents as well. LIC has also put in place facilities of internet payments, electronic clearing system, ATMs, etc. LIC has also put in place a massive data warehousing system in house IT system thus providing tremendous support to management decisions and improving service quality with speed.

Conclusion

The above discussion indicates that LIC has made relevant changes in its marketing strategies in the post liberalised era to face the challenges put up by liberalisation. Most important change observed is a professionalism, which has become the way of operations for LIC. The entire transformation in the post liberalized era revolved around 'Product Variety, Service and Professionalism'. LIC has developed products to provide for every life insurance related need of customers and further it is innovating more and more customized products. Also LIC has set up 'Claims Review Committees' at Central and Zonal Levels, comprising of experienced LIC officials and legal experts. Also LIC is beefing up its human resources, instilling a professional outlook in areas such as customer focus and risk management, providing both on the job and classroom training and also delegating power to lower officer for faster claims and grievance settlement. On the infrastructure front LIC is leaving no stone unturned and is committed to provide service excellence through technology. LIC is actively utilizing the internet medium for the purpose of sales distribution and also it is making efforts to lead in the business through alternate channel. LIC is concentrating efforts in training its manpower at best of institutes and training and product development has become a continuous exercise at LIC, Thus the comparison of strategies of LIC in the pre and post liberalized era seem to give a picture of an immense change and a positive change from a monopoly operation to a competitive and highly professionalized operation.

REFERENCES

1. Customer Service Center (2003), "The Under Development Asset for Customer Retention, Loyalty and Revenue Enhancing Strategies", *Insurance White Paper* (www.knowlagent.com).
2. Dayal, Ishwar, (1992), "Reorganisation of LIC—A Rewarding Experience", *Yogakshema,* pp. 17-18 and 25.
3. Debasish S. (2004), "Exploring Customer Preference for Life Insurance in India—Factor Analysis Method", *Vilakshan-XIMB Journal of Management,* Vol. 1, No. I, March, pp. 7-15.
4. Dhanda, R.L. (2004), "Divisional Performance Evaluation of LIC Business in Northern Zone", *Finance India,* Vol. XVIII, No. 1, pp. 229-33.
5. Dhunna, Mukesh and Rajan, A.K. (2002), "Liberalization of Insurance Sector: Social Implications", *Indian Management Studies Journal,* Vol. 6, pp. 109-117.
6. Aggarwal, Preeti (2005), "A Note on the Insurance Status in India for *Poor", Alliance Journal of Business Research,* pp. 35-45.
7. Ahuja, Rajeev (2004), "Even Development—Reaching Rural Areas and the Socially Weak", *IRDA Journal,* Vol. III, No. 1, pp. 28-29.
8. Ahuja, Rajeev (2004), "Insurance: Over the Transition", *Economic and Political Weekly,* Vol. 35, No. 32, August 7, Mumbai, pp. 3569.
9. Annual Reports of Life Insurance Corporation of India for different years.
10. Jawaharlal, U. and N. Pareek (2004), "Customer Service in Life Insurance", *Insurance Chronicle,* Vol. IV, Issue IV, pp. 17-19.
11. Johri, Govind, 'Customer Satisfaction in Emerging Insurance Market in India'; *The Insurance Times,* October 2000, p. 21.
12. Joshi (2003), "Changing Customer Expectations in Insurance Sector—Pre to Post Liberalization", IRDA—FORTE Conference on Consumer Awareness: Insurance Sector, Study Conducted By MART for FORTE and IRDA.
13. Kalra, R.K. and D.K. Garg (1999), "AIDA Model and Rural Marketing with Special Reference to LIC Policies", *Management Stream,* Vol. 1, No. 1, pp. 56-59.

SECTION–II

HUMAN RESOURCE MANAGEMENT

CHAPTER

7

Training and Development : A Key to Success in Hospitality Sector

Prof. Basant Mehta
Mrs. Priyanka Choudhary

ABSTRACT

Hospitality is about serving the guests to provide them with "feel-good-effect". *"Athithi devo bhavha"* (Guest is God) has been one of central creed of Indian culture since times immemorial. In India, the guest is treated with utmost warmth and respect and is provided the best services. Today hospitality sector is one of the fastest growing sectors in India. It is expected to grow at the rate of 8% between 2007 and 2016. The training and development activities are now equally important with that of other HR functions. Gone are the days, when training was considered to be futile, waste of time, resources, and money. Now-a-days, training are an investment because the departments such as, marketing and sales, HR, production, finance, etc depends on training for its survival. Training is now the important tool of Human Resource Management to control the attrition rate because it helps in motivating employees, achieving their professional and personal goals, increasing the level of job satisfaction, etc. As a result training is given on a variety of skill development to the employees.

Key Words: *Human Resource Management., Training and Development, Hospitality Sector, Employee Development.*

Introduction

The HR functioning is changing with time and with this change, the relationship between the training function and other management activity is also changing. The training and development activities are now equally important with that of other HR functions. If training is not considered as a priority or not seen as a vital part in the organization, then it is difficult to accept that such a company has effectively carried out HRM. Training actually provides the opportunity to raise the profile development activities in the organization.

HRM require careful planning as well as greater emphasis on employee development and long term education. Training is now the important tool of Human Resource Management to control the attrition rate because it helps in motivating employees, achieving their professional and personal goals, increasing the level of job satisfaction, etc. These major players are now strategizing to increase the turnover of the customers by training their employees on Communication, Dining and Business etiquettes, etc.

- Good infrastructure
- Trained trainer
- Quality of content
- Certification of training course
- Effective training evaluation

Training and Development Programmes are available for the following areas:

- Food Production
- Food and Beverage Service

- Front Office
- Housekeeping

Training: It is a learning process that involves the acquisition of knowledge, sharpening of skills, concepts, rules, or changing of attitudes and behaviours to enhance the performance of employees. Training is activity leading to skilled behaviour.

- It's not what you want in life, but it's knowing how to reach it
- It's not where you want to go, but it's knowing how to get there
- It's not how high you want to rise, but it knows how to take off
- It may not be quite the outcome you were aiming for, but it will be an outcome
- It's not what you dream of doing, but it's having the knowledge to do it
- It's not a set of goals, but it's more like a vision

It's not the goal you set, but it's what you need to achieve it.

Training is about knowing where you stand (no matter how good or bad the current situation looks) at present, and where you will be after some point of time. Training is about the acquisition of knowledge, skills, and abilities (KSA) through professional development.

Training Required Entering Hotel Industry

Candidates can enter the hotel industry through different means. Vocational Training given for positions of room attendants, cooks, receptionists, bellboys, people working in the bakery etc.

Role of Training

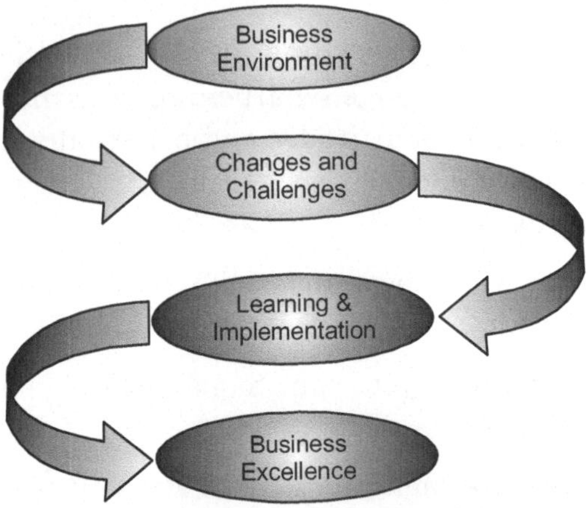

Importance of Training and Development

- **Optimum Utilization of Human Resources :** Training and Development helps in optimizing the utilization of human resource that further helps the employee to achieve the organizational goals as well as their individual goals.
- **Image :** Training and Development helps in creating a better corporate image.
- **Profitability :** Training and Development leads to improved profitability and more positive attitudes towards profit orientation.
- Training and Development aids in organizational development i.e. Organization gets more effective decision-making and problem solving. It helps in understanding and carrying out organizational policies.
- Training and Development helps in developing leadership skills, motivation, loyalty, better attitudes, and other aspects that successful workers and managers usually display.

Importance of Training Objectives

Training objectives are one of the most important parts of training programme. While some people think of training objective as a waste of valuable time. It provides the clear guidelines and develops the training programme in less time because objectives focus specifically on needs. It helps in adhering to a plan. Training objective tell the trainee that what is expected out of him at the end of the training programme. Training objectives are of great significance from a number of stakeholder perspectives

1. Trainer
2. Trainee
3. Designer
4. Evaluator

Trainer : The training objective is also beneficial to trainer because it helps the trainer to measure the progress of trainees and make the required adjustments. Also, trainer comes in a position to establish a relationship between objectives and particular segments of training.

- **Development of human resources** : Training and Development helps to provide an opportunity and broad structure for the development of human resources' technical and behavioural skills in an organization. It also helps the employees in attaining personal growth.
- **Development of skills of employees** : Training and Development helps in increasing the job knowledge and skills of employees at each level. It helps to expand the horizons of human intellect and an overall personality of the employees.
- **Productivity** : Training and Development helps in increasing the productivity of the employees that helps the organization further to achieve its long-term goal.

- **Team spirit** : Training and Development helps in inculcating the sense of team work, team spirit, and inter-team collaborations. It helps in inculcating the zeal to learn within the employees.
- **Organization culture** : Training and Development helps to develop and improve the organizational health culture and effectiveness. It helps in creating the learning culture within the organization.
- **Organization climate** : Training and Development helps building the positive perception and feeling about the organization. The employees get these feelings from leaders, subordinates, and peers.
- **Quality** : Training and Development helps in improving upon the quality of work and work-life.
- **Healthy work environment** : Training and Development helps in creating the healthy working environment. It helps to build good employee, relationship so that individual goals aligns with organizational goal.
- **Health and safety** : Training and Development helps in improving the health and safety of the organization thus preventing obsolescence.
- **Morale** : Training and Development helps in improving the morale of the work force.

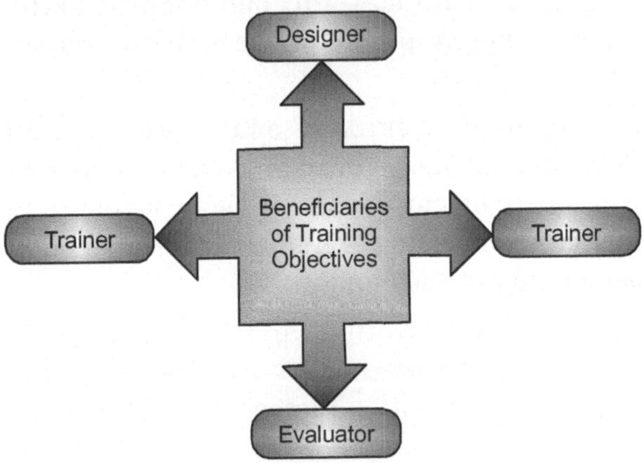

Trainee : The training objective is beneficial to the trainee because it helps in reducing the anxiety of the trainee up to some extent. Not knowing anything or going to a place which is unknown creates anxiety that can negatively affect learning. Therefore, it is important to keep the participants aware of the happenings, rather than keeping it surprise. Secondly, it helps in increase in concentration, which is the crucial factor to make the training successful. The objectives create an image of the training programme in trainee's mind that actually helps in gaining attention. Thirdly, if the goal is set to be challenging and motivating, then the likelihood of achieving those goals is much higher than the situation in which no goal is set. Therefore, training objectives helps in increasing the probability that the participants will be successful in training.

Designer : The training objective is beneficial to the training designer because if the designer is aware what is to be achieved in the end then he'll buy the training package according to that only. The training designer would then look for the training methods, training equipments, and training content accordingly to achieve those objectives. Furthermore, planning always helps in dealing effectively in an unexpected situation. Consider an example; the objective of one training programme is to deal effectively with customers to increase the sales. Since the objective is known, the designer will design a training programme that will include ways to improve the interpersonal skills, such as verbal and non verbal language, dealing in unexpected situation i.e. when there is a defect in a product or when a customer is angry. Therefore, without any guidance, the training may not be designed appropriately.

Evaluator : It becomes easy for the training evaluator to measure the progress of the trainees because the objectives define the expected performance of trainees. Training objective is an important to tool to judge the performance of participants.

Role of HRD Professionals in Training

This is the era of cut-throat competition and with this changing scenario of business; the role of HR professionals in training has been widened. HR role now is:

1. Active involvement in employee education;
2. Rewards for improvement in performance;
3. Rewards to be associated with self esteem and self worth;
4. Providing pre-employment market oriented skill development education and post employment support for advanced education and training; and
5. Flexible access i.e. anytime, anywhere training.

Opportunities in Hospitality Industry

The government is making tremendous effort in the areas of investment and infrastructure with an overall aim to boost the tourism industry. At the present growth rate, the sector is very healthy and the boom will continue. The industry is growing at a very rapid pace and there is a demand for more rooms both in metres and smaller towns. The hospitality industry is intricately linked to the tourism industry and the growth in the Indian tourism industry has fuelled the growth of the Indian hotel industry. The current growth of the hospitality industry has been driven by three main factors:

- The middle class segment in India is growing and Indians are becoming more mobile within and outside the country;
- India has become the IT centre of Asia bringing in more investment; and
- The Indian Ministry of Tourism has been proactive in launching a successful global advertising campaign' Incredible India'. There is no doubt that the hospitality industry is going to grow by leaps and bounds in the near future. There are better prospects in store, all thanks to the growing tourism industry.

Soft Skills Needed in Hospitality Sector

The important soft skills that one must possess is the ability to listen patiently to customer needs, and be calm at the same time have the analytical mind to find what needs to be done at that very moment.

Front Office

How you greet a guest the moment he arrives, how you help him with the initial formalities all comprise the basic tenets of soft skills that you need to master fast. Other important areas that need training are communication etiquettes like how to shake hands, and a positive body language both of which go a long way in reinforcing the fact that you are giving your guest undivided attention.

Restaurant

Here, what cardinally matters is how you welcome the guest and make him feel comfortable. If the guest has visited the restaurant previously, remembering his name or his likes and dislikes are extremely crucial. To surprise of many, even presentation of food requires soft skills. In food production, how you garnish the salad, how you make food, look and smell better also come under the purview of soft skills. Broadly, all employees must know how to deal with customers firmly yet tactfully at times. Sometimes a guest may misbehave with a female staff member.

Conclusion

Training is the important tool of Human Resource Management to control the attrition rate in hotel industry because it helps in motivating employees, achieving their professional and personal goals, increasing the level of job satisfaction. As a result training is given on a variety of skill development to the employees. It helps the industry, to achieve its long term goal by increasing the productivity of employees, inculcating the sense of team work and team spirit and developing the positive work climate. Therefore training and development imparts belter prospects to the growing tourism industry in India.

REFERENCES

Books and Journals

Blum C. Shane (1996) "Organizational Trend Analysis of the Hospitality Industry: *Preparing for Change"* Volume 8, p. 20-32, ISSN: 1959-6119.

Davies Eddie (2003) *"The Training Manager's—A Handbook"* Publisher: Crest Publishing House, New Delhi.

Deva Vasu (2002) *"Training and Development"* Publisher: Commonwealth Publishers, New Delhi.

Harris J. Kimberley (1995) *"Training Technology in the Hospitality Industry: A Matter of Effectiveness and Efficiency"* Volume 7, p. 24-29, ISSN: 1959-6119.

Lyton P. Rolf and Pareek Udai (1990) "Training and Development" Publisher: *Vistaar,* New Delhi.

Mulcahy D. John (1999) *"Vocational Work Experience in the Hospitality Industry: Characteristics and Strategies"* Volume 41, p. 164-174, ISSN 0040-0912.

Rao P.L (2001) *"HRD Through In-House Training"* Publisher: ISTD, Vikas Publishing House, New Delhi.

Robinson R. Kenneth (1988) *"A Handbook of Training Management"* publisher: Aditya Book Pvt. Ltd., New Delhi.

Washington Keithen, Fienstein Hale Andrew and Busser A. James(2003) *"Evaluating the Effect of Training on Perceptions of Internal Occupational Status"* Volume 22, Issue 3, p. 243-265.

Web Sites:

- www.ezinearticles.com
- www. bestwestern.com
- www.hospitalitybizz.com
- www.managementhelp.org

CHAPTER

8

Personnel Management in Indian Banks with Context of Public and Private Sector Banks

Prof. Basant Mehta
Dr. Mrs. Shruti Kanthalia

INTRODUCTION

The present study compares the personnel management philosophy, policies and practices in public and private sector bank with special reference to SBBJ and IDBI which represent public and private sector banks respectively. Personnel Management or Human Resource Management Plays a crucial role in the development process of economics. The level of development of most of the economies is dependent upon the level of development of human resources. In fact, it is said that all development comes from the human mind. Personnel Management is responsible for the transformation of traditional economies into modern and industrial economies. Successful management depends upon the management of human behaviour. If an organisation is successful, it means it is efficient at the management of its human resources.

Personnel Management plays a vital role in a service oriented industry like banks. In India, banks are important financial institutions for achieving economic development and social upliftment. The banking scene in the country has undergone a massive change since the nationalization of commercial banks.

The banking industry has grown not only in terms of size of its operation and the number of bank branches, but also in terms of its functional diversification. This multidimensional growth was accomplished by many organisational changes. It also necessitated sound management of human resources.

Thus, in view of changing scenario also it can be concluded that Personnel Management assumes greater significance in a service oriented industry like banks. The Personnel Management function must be recognized as a separate activity with the view to recruit qualified persons in the banks and to ensure their career development, enhance their administrative capacity, motivate them to contribute their best and to improve the overall efficiency of the banking system. It is very much necessary to have a properly designed central machinery in all the banks for human resource development.

Sampling Design

Primary data is collected through Questionnaires and Personal Interview. Secondary data is collected from periodicals, government reports, annual reports of banks, past studies and research papers and was also taken from various websites. The data collected from the primary and secondary sources were analyzed by using appropriate mathematical and statistical tools such as Percentage, Z-Test, and Chi Square Test.

Sampling design is definite plan for obtaining a sample from a given population. It refers to a technique a sample and the sample size.

In I stage sampling the sampling frame consisted of a list of all the public and private sector commercial banks in the district which is taken from bankers club, Udaipur. Two sample commercial banks, each from public sector and private sector banks, were selected. SBBJ representing public sector and IDBI representing private sector were taken as sample banks.

In II stage sampling respondents were to be selected from both the banks. Sampling frame consisted of the list of bank employees which is for the purpose of choosing a random sample. From this list a sample random sample of 100 respondent was drawn for both banks which is considered as sufficient for the purpose of the study as well as for analysis. The same number of employees has been taken to avoid inaccurate and unbiased judgment. Thus the total size of 200 has been taken from both the banks.

Main Findings of the Study

The present study consists of sample size of 100 employees each from SBBJ and IDBI from whom responses were collected through questionnaire. For comparative analysis between the samples profiles of both banks Z test was used which revealed the following facts.

(*i*) The age-wise profile shows that no significant difference exists between the two banks in the age group of 21-30, 31-40, and above 50 years whereas significant difference exists in the age group of 41-50 years.

(*ii*) The gender-wise profile shows that no significant difference exists between the two banks.

(*iii*) Cast-wise profile shows that no significant difference exists between the two banks regarding the different castes of the respondents.

(*iv*) Education-wise profile shows that no significant difference exists between the two banks regarding education level of HSC, post Graduate, MBA, CAICS/ICWA, and any other whereas significant difference exists in the education of Graduate level.

(*v*) Profile of respondents on the basis of length of service shows that no significant difference exists between the two banks regarding length of service for period upto 5 yrs, 6-10, 11-15 years whereas significant difference exists in the length of service ranging in between 16- 20 years and more than 20 years.

Findings on comparative analysis between SBBJ and IDBI on the basis of Personnel Management policies and practices followed by both the banks:

1. **Recruitment** : On the whole no difference was found between SBBJ and IDBI regarding the source of recruitment in both the banks. It is found that majority of the respondents in both the banks i.e. 76% respondents of SBBJ and 80% respondents of IDBI were recruited through advertisements. While 16% employees of SBBJ and 16% employees of IDBI were recruited through employment exchange and reference respectively. 92% respondents of SBBJ and 80% respondents of IDBI are of the view that, advertisement is the best method to recruit employees.
2. **Selection** : In both the banks i.e. SBBJ and IDBI, the selection procedure started with the screening of application for selection and rejection of candidates is practiced. Most of the selection was done for entry level jobs, because higher level jobs were filled mainly through promotion. In SBBJ, employees were selected by the Banking Service-Recruitment Board (BSRB) While IDBI-have its own board which selects employees. It was observed that after the abolition of recruitment board in the year 2000, no fresh recruitment have been made by SBBJ, Research findings showed that 92% respodents of SBBJ and 80% respondents of IDBI were selected on the basis of written test and interview. 58% respondents of SBBJ and 40% respondents of IDBI were satisfied with selection procedure because it is based on merit. 52% respondents of SBBJ and 36% respondents of IDBI feel that their academic qualification was helpful in their selection. The probation period of 60% respondents of SBBJ and 70% respondents of IDBI was between 6 months to 1 year While the probation period of 24% respondents of SBBJ and 28% respondents of IDBI was between six months to one

year. To compare the selection practices in both the banks chi sq test was conducted and it is proved that no significant difference exists between the two banks regarding the selection practices in SBBJ and IDBI.

3. **Training :** Nearly 50% respondents of both the banks attended 1-2 training programmers While rest 50% respondents of both the banks attended more than three training programmers in between their service period. The respondents were interested in getting training in the filed of management, marketing, personnel, finance and information technology. To compare the training given in SBBJ and IDBI chi sq test was conducted and it proved statistically that no significant difference was found between both the banks on the basis of training given to employees in both the banks.

4. **Salary and Bonus :** Salary is a major motivation for any employees to perform better. On the whole it was found that no difference exists between the salary structure of SBBJ and IDBI. Regarding bonus, in SBBJ it was given to an employees whose salary was more than Rs. 8500/- and in IDBI there is no such minimum amount of salary for receiving bonus as all the employees get the bonus yearly.

   The findings reveal that in SBBJ none of the respondents was getting bonus but in IDBI majority of the respondents i.e. (90%) gets the bonus. In comparison to SBBJ more respondents in IDBI were of the opinion that salary given to them was adequate considering the nature of their job. The findings shows that both the banks provide almost the same type of allowance like medical, LTC, entertainment allowance on fixed basis while petrol, Telephone allowance on actual basis. To compare the research finding on salary in SBBJ and IDBI chi sq test was conducted and it proved statistically that no significant difference was found between SBBJ and IDBI regarding salary given to employees.

5. **Fring Benefits** : The only difference is in the quantum of amount which is more in IDBI as compared to SBBJ.
6. **Promotion** : There was a vast difference in both the banks regarding the number of respondent who were promoted About 44% and 100% respondent in SBBJ and IDBI respectively received promotion. In both the banks employees were promoted sometimes on merit basis on seniority basis and also merit cum seniority basis. The main reason for respondents i.e. 60% of IDBI and 54% of SBBJ not being promoted was that they didn't want to be promoted. Other reason like no vacancy at higher level or not trained etc. also existed. Most of the respondents were of the view that timely promotion generally increased their efficiency of working and monetary benefits, along with job satisfaction. In comparison to 46% respondents of SBBJ, more respondents i.e. 62% of IDBI were satisfied with the present promotion policy of banks. To compare the promotion practices in SBBJ and IDBI chi sq test was conducted and it proved statistically that significant difference exist between the two banks especially with regard to the number of employees promoted and the basis on which they were promoted.
7. **Transfer** : It was found that 90% respondents were transferred in IDBI in comparison to 68% respondents of SBBJ. Those respondents who were transferred, among them the main cause of transfer was the promotion policy. It was found that majority of the respondents in both the banks i.e. 62% of IDBI and 53% of SBBJ were of the view that transfer increased their ability to work. 27% of IDBI and 29% respondents of SBBJ say that transfer has no effect on their working ability. Regarding nature of transfer majority of the respondents in both the banks i.e. 48% of IDBI and 36% of SBBJ were of the view that

transfer provides them creative opportunities at other place. Both banks also transfer their employees i.e. 28% of IDBI and 32% of SBBJ to increase the banks effectiveness or to correct erroneous placements and for temporary adjustments also. But on the whole no significant difference exists between SBBJ and IDBI with regards to transfer policy.

8. **Separation :** In both SBBJ and IDBI the employees are mainly separated as a result of resignation, retirement, dismissal or suspension. Recently, SBBJ introduced a new scheme called Voluntary Retirement Scheme (VRS) to down size its staff strength. Yet, IDBI has so far not introduced any VRS scheme for its employees.

The research findings showed that in both the banks majority of the respondents were not interested in taking VRS had this been offered to them. Increased monetary benefits and preference for other job were found to be the main reasons behind some of the employees desiring VRS.

To compare the research finding on VRS in SBBJ and IDBI, chi sq test was conducted and it proved statistically that no significant difference exists between both the banks on the basis of respondents' opinion regarding VRS. On the Whole the researcher observed that in SBBJ, VRS outgo had substantially reduced the declared profits of banks. Also, shortfall of bank staff was observed. In a bank like SBBJ, which is still facing the Problems of non performing assets, hasty implementation of substantive policies had made the matter worse.

IV. Testing of Hypothesis

The result of this investigation approves our following hypothesis :

(*a*) "Advertisement is the best method of recruitment then any other method of Recruitment."

(*b*) "Training and Orientation programmers are organized and attended more in public sector banks as compared to private sector banks."

(*c*) "Salary administration and fringe benefits are better in private sector banks as compared to public sector banks."

(*d*) "Promotion opportunities are more in private sector banks as compared to public sector."

V. Suggestions

1. 80% respondents of SBBJ and 78% respondents of IDBI 'files reference' is the worst method of recruitment while 16% respondents of SBBJ and 12% respondents of IDBI also fires employee referrals is the worst method of recruitment so it is suggested that proper sources of recruitment should be there with a proper reorientation of recruitment policies. Therefore both SBBJ and IDBI should establish a link with educational institutions as the educational set ups have not so far devised a comprehensive course aimed at the students, who wish to become a bank employee. Banks should, therefore, give a serious thought to persuading educational institutions to introduce banking education as part of their curriculum. To begin with, a tie up with Indian Institute of Management and other management institutes of repute could be considered.
2. 30% respondents of SBBJ and 22% respondents of IDBI are of the view that induction information given to them was not sufficient so it is suggested that both the banks should use other methods like management films to give induction information to their employees.
3. Training course in banks should cover new areas like merchant banking, investment consultancy, tax planning, information technology, etc. training facilities should be such that the respondents should develop a spirit of initiative, innovation and service orientation in place of the present attitude of indifference and lethargy.

4. Salary given to employees should be linked with the performance of the employees even it may alter according to performance.
5. Bonus is given to employees in SBBJ whose salary is more than Rs. 8,500/- so it is suggested that this, 'limit should be dropped and the percentage of the bonus should be increased and bonus should be given to all employees in proportion to their salary.

REFERENCES

Arya and Yash Pal, *Research Methodology in Management,* Deep & Deep Publications, 2001.

Arya, P.P. & Tandon H., *Human Resource Development,* Deep & Deep, New Delhi, 1991.

Basu, C.R., *Human Resource Development,* Indian Journal of Commerce, Vol. XI (Jan-June 1997).

Basu, K.S., *New Dimension in Personnel Management,* McMillan, 1979.

C.B. Gupta, *Principles of Management for Bankers,* Sultan Chand & Sons, 1994.

Chatterjee, N.N., *Management of Personnel in Indian Enterprises,* Allied Book Agency, Calcutta.

Ghotgalkar, R.K., *Service Condition of Bank Employees,* Himalaya Publishers House.

Kohli Udesh & Sinha, D.P., *Human Resource Development Global Changes and Strategies in 2000 A.D.,* Allied, New Delhi, 1994.

Mehta Basant, Kothari Kiran, *Human Resource Management,* Vol. I & II, Discovery Publishing House, New Delhi, 1999.

Mehta Basant, Jain Pragya, *Role of Banks in Women Development,* Discovery Publishing House, New Delhi, 2003.

Mehta Basant, Kanthalia Shruti, *Personnel Management in Banks,* Discovery Publishing House, New Delhi, 2008.

Michael, V.P., *Research Methodology in Management,* Himalaya, Bombay, 1985.

P. Subba Rao, *Principles and Practice of Bank Management,* Himalaya Publishing House, 1994.

Prasad Lal, *Personnel Management and Industrial Relations in Public Sector,* Progressive Publishing, Bombay, 1973.

Singh and Bhattacharya, *Banking Sector Management,* Discovery Publishing House, Delhi, 1990.

Singh, A.K., *Personnel Management in Public Enterprises,* Mittal, 1985.

Subbarao, P., *Principles and Practice of Bank Management,* Himalaya Publishing House.

Subhas Kumar, *Manpower Planning in SBI, Classical Publishing Company,* 2000.

Vasant Desai, *Principles of Bank Management,* Himalaya Publishing House, Mumbai.

Annual Reports

Annual Reports of State Bank of Bikaner and Jaipur (SBBJ). Annual Reports of Industrial Development Bank of India (IDBI).

WEBSITES

www.sbbibank.com
www.idbibank.com
www.iiborg.in
www.sbi.org.in
www.bankersindia.com
www.indiabudjet.nic.in
www.hindutimes.com
www.rajasthaninfoline.com
www.asiabusinesstoday.org

CHAPTER

9

Teamwork Your Way To Success

Prof. Basant Mehta
Ms. Priyanka Choudhary

ABSTRACT

A team is any group of people organized to work together interdependently and cooperatively to meet the needs of their customers by accomplishing a purpose and goals. Teams are created for both long-term and short-term interaction. A product development team, an executive leadership team, and a departmental team are long lasting planning and operational groups. Short-term teams might include a team to develop an employee on boarding process, a team to plan the annual company party, or a team to respond to a specific customer problem or complaint. People in every workplace talk about team building, working as a team, and my team, but few understand how to create the experience of team building or how to develop an effective team. Many view teams as the best organization design for involving all employees in creating business success and profitability. Learn how team building helps enable the success of work teams and team work.

Team building is a process of awareness building. It's helping people to understand that they are greater collectively than individually. It is an understanding that all of our decisions will be better when some degree of collaboration is applied. People in every workplace talk about team building, how to create effective teams, team work, and team building is a challenge in every organization.

Key Words: *Team Building, Effective Teams, Success and Profitability.*

"Praise publicly, correct privately. Ask for input on decisions which affect others—and use it. Credit others when praise is thrown your way. Focus on the positives in your teammates and their negatives will begin to fade."

What is a Team : A team is any group of people organized to work together interdependently and cooperatively to meet the needs of their customers by accomplishing a purpose and goals. Teams are created for both long-term and short-term interaction. A product development team, an executive leadership team, and a departmental team are long lasting planning and operational groups. Short-term teams might include a team to develop an employee on boarding process, a team to plan the annual company party, or a team to respond to a specific customer problem or complaint. Three common types of teams include functional or departmental, cross-functional, and self-managing.

- **Functional or departmental teams :** Groups of people from the same work area or department, who meet on a regular basis to analyze customer needs, solve problems, provide members with support, promote continuous improvement, and share information.
- **Cross-functional teams :** Groups of people who are pulled together from across departments or job functions to deal with a specific product, issue, customer, problem, or to improve a particular process.
- **Self-managing teams :** Groups of people who gradually assume responsibility for self-direction in all aspects of work.

Team Building

Team building is a process of awareness building. It's helping people to understand that they are greater collectively than individually. It is an understanding that all of our decisions will be better when some degree of collaboration is applied. It is bringing people to a place where there is an honest appreciation of each other's essence...where they come from...where they've been. Because in this appreciation is the driver for collaboration.

Twelve Cs for Team Building

Executives, managers and organization staff members universally explore ways to improve business results and profitability. Many view team-based, horizontal, organization structures as the best design for involving all employees in creating business success. Few organizations, however, are totally pleased with the results their team improvement efforts produce. If your team improvement efforts are not living up to your expectations, this self-diagnosing checklist may tell you why. Successful team building, that creates effective, focussed work teams, requires attention to each of the following.

- **Clear Expectations:** Executive leadership has clearly communicated its expectations for the team's performance and expected outcomes. Team members do understand why the team was created. And the organization is demonstrating constancy of purpose in supporting the team with resources of people, time and money.
- **Context:** Team members understand why they are participating on the team: they understand how the strategy of using teams will help the organization attain its communicated business goals; they define their team's importance to the accomplishment of corporate goals. And the team understands where its work fits in the total context of the organization's goals, principles, vision and values.
- **Commitment:** Members committed to accomplishing the team mission and expected outcomes. And they perceive their service as valuable to the organization

and to their own careers; anticipate recognition for their contributions; expect their skills to grow and develop on the team.

- **Competence:** The team feels that it has the appropriate people participating. And their members have the knowledge, skill and capability to address the issues for which the team was formed; the team feels it has the resources, strategies and support needed to accomplish its mission.
- **Charter:** The team has taken its assigned area of responsibility and designed its own mission, vision and strategies to accomplish the mission. And defined and communicated its goals; its anticipated outcomes and contributions; its timelines; and how it will measure both the outcomes of its work and the process the team followed to accomplish their task.
- **Control:** The team has enough freedom and empowerment to feel the ownership necessary to accomplish its charter. At the same time, the team members clearly understand their boundaries. The organization has a plan to increase opportunities for self-management among organization members.
- **Collaboration:** The team understands team and group process. Members understand the stages of group development, roles and responsibilities of team members, team leaders, and team recorders. The team established group norms or rules of conduct in areas such as conflict resolution, consensus decision making and meeting management. And using an appropriate strategy to accomplish its action plan.
- **Communication:** Team members clear about the priority of their tasks. There is an established method for the teams to give feedback and receive honest performance feedback. The organization provides important business information regularly and teams understand the complete context for their existence.

- **Creative Innovation:** The organization is really interested in change. It creates value creative thinking, unique solutions, and new ideas. It rewards people who take reasonable risks to make improvements. And it provides the training, education, access to books and films, and field trips necessary to stimulate new thinking.
- **Consequences:** Team members feel responsible and accountable for team achievements. Team members spend their time finger pointing rather than resolving problems, the organization designing reward systems that recognize both team and individual performance. The organization is planning to share gains and increased profitability with team and individual contributors.
- **Coordination:** Teams are coordinated by a central leadership team that assists the groups to obtain what they need for success. And have priorities and resource allocation been planned across departments.
- **Cultural Change:** The organization recognizes that the team-based, collaborative, empowering, enabling organizational culture of the future is different than the traditional, hierarchical organization. The organization is planning to or in the process of changing how it rewards, recognizes, appraises, hires, develops, plans with, motivates and manages the people.

The Path to Team Building Success

How to create effective teams, team work, and team building is a challenge in every organization. Work environments tend to foster rugged individuals working on personal goals for personal gain. Typically, reward, recognition, and pay systems single out the achievements of individual employees.

Appraisal, performance management, and goal setting systems most frequently focus on individual goals and progress, not on team building. Promotions and additional authority are also bestowed on individuals. Given these factors, it is wonder that teams and team work are an uphill battle in most organizations.

Teams

Employee involvement, teams, and employee empowerment enable people to make decisions about their work. This employee involvement, team building approach, and employee empowerment increases loyalty and fosters ownership. These resources tell you how to do team building and effectively involve people.

Employee Empowerment: How to Empower Employees

Employee empowerment is a strategy and philosophy that enables employees to make decisions about their jobs. Employee empowerment helps employees own their work and take responsibility for their results.

Employee Involvement: Involve Employees in Decision-making

Employee involvement is creating an environment in which people has an impact on decisions and actions that affect their jobs Employee involvement is a management and leadership philosophy about how people are enabled to contribute to continuous improvement and the ongoing success of their organization.

Team Building Creates Successful Teams

People in every workplace talk about team building, working as a team, and my team, but few understand how to create the experience of team building or how to develop an effective team. Many view teams as the best organization design for involving all employees in creating business success and profitability. Learn how team building helps enable the success of work teams and team work.

Teams and Team Building Resources

Find recommended reading to create effective work teams, successful team work, and team building ideas and activities.

Meeting Management for Team Meetings

Ineffective team meetings use critical resources, sap organizational energy and movement, and affect employee morale. Find out how to make your team meetings work.

Team Building Holidays

Find ideas for successful teams, effective team work, and team building around holiday ideas and themes.

Positive Work Relationships Contribute to Effective Teams

Positive relationship with teams, supervisor, manager, customer or coworker makes interpersonal relationships positive, supportive, clear, and empowering.

Phases of a Team's Development

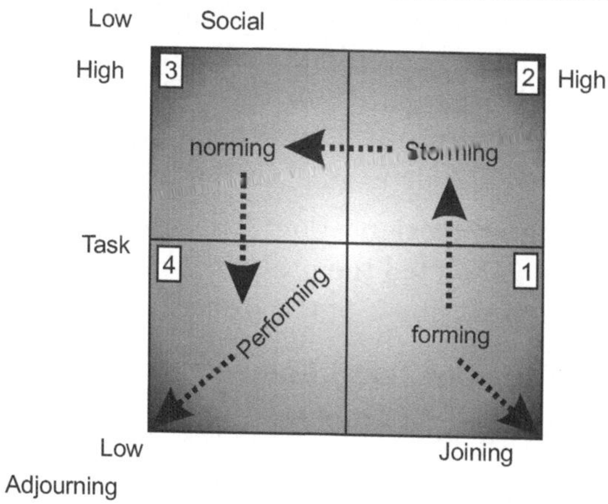

A team is a living and dynamic entity.. It could progress from an early to a mature phase, independent of the nature of the team or the task it must perform.

Forming : This is the initial orientation period. The team is unsure about what it is supposed to do members do not know each other well or are not yet familiar with the way the team leader and the other members function. This stage is complete when the members begin to see themselves as a part of the group.

Storming : This is a sorting out period where members begin to find their place as team members. The team members now feel more comfortable giving their opinion and challenging the team leader's authority and recommendations. Some members may become dissatisfied and challenge not only the tasks of the team and how these will be carried out, but also the leader's role and style of leadership. This is the start of intragroup conflicts.

Norming : Team members begin to use their past experiences to solve their problems and pull together as a cohesive group. This process should result in the team establishing procedures for handling conflicts, decisions, and methods to accomplish the team projects.

Performing: In this phase the team has achieved harmony, defined its tasks, worked out its relationships, and has started producing results. Leadership is provided by the team member's best suited for the task at hand. Members have learned how to work together, manage conflict and contribute their resources to meet the team's purposes.

Dissolving or reorientation: The team dissolves when the team has completed the project. It may be reoriented to continue on a next phase of the project.

Responsibilities of Team Leader

- Assign clear tasks to each member
- Regularly review and monitor progress of work
- Ensure that the team meets deadlines
- Discuss and agree on the timetable for major activities with the team

- Motivate team members
- Resolve conflicts
- Give guidance when needed
- Helps members to overcome barriers
- Regularly assess team performance using a checklist

Why Teams Fail

Some teams fail from the beginning and some deteriorate over time. Given below are the most relevant external and internal barriers to team success. These may help to identify the development and support needs of members that may impact on the success of teams.

External Barriers to Teamwork

- Work load: members are often required to work on their team assignments in addition to a full workload or are given more work than they are capable of handling.
- Inadequate recognition for individual team members.
- Team leaders do not control or release the team members adequately.
- Teams are not given adequate resources.
- Frequent changes in team membership.

Internal Barriers to Teamwork

- Inadequate support from key external stakeholders.
- Team members don't set appropriate goals for the team and do not implement a plan for reaching them.
- Team members don't spend enough time planning how they will work together.
- Team members don't resolve interpersonal conflict.
- Team members don't have compatible levels of problem-solving, analytic, or project management skills.

Conclusion

Team building and planning events and activities have the potential to bring the people employ a strong sense of direction, workable plans and solutions, a powerful feeling of belonging with and on the team and clear, strategic customer-focussed values. Poorly planned and executed, created outside of the context of the total organization, the team building and planning sessions bring disappointment, low morale and negative motivation.

REFERENCES

- Boss, R. Wayne; McConkie, Mark L. (1981), *"The Destructive Impact of Positive Team Building Intervention".* Volume 6 No. 1, 45-56.
- Cameron, Klein, Deborah Diaz Granados (2009), *"Does Team Building Work",* Volume 40 No. 2, 181-222.
- Joan R. Rentsch, Tonia S. Heffner (1994), *"What You Know Is What You Get From Experience",* Volume 19 No. 4, 450-474.
- Kimberly A., Smith-Jentsch, Janis A. Cannon-Bowers (2008), *"Guided Team Self-Correction",* Volume 39 No. 3, 303-327.
- Paul K. Buller (1986), *"The Team Building-Task Performance Relation: Some Conceptual and Methodological Refinements"* Volume 11 No. 3, 147-168.
- Richard Klimoski, Susan Mohammed (1994), *"Team Mental Model: Construct or Metaphor",* Volume 20 No. 2, 403-437.
- Sundstrom, Eric, De Meuse, Kenneth P. Futrell David (1990), *"Work Teams: Applications and Effectiveness"*Volume 45, No. 2, 120-133.

WEB SITES

- www.tearnbuildingusa.com
- www.businessballs.com
- www.online.sagepub.com
- www.ezinearticles.com

CHAPTER

10

Training Programme in Public and Private Sector Bank

Prof. Basant Mehta
Dr. (Mrs.) Shruti Khanthalia

Introduction

The bank and the employees is expected to develop and progress simultaneously for the attainment of mutual goals. This could be made possible through HRD. In its endeavour, bank management needs to adopt the modern technique which includes training. Training of an employee is a specialised function and said to be one of the fundamental operative functions of personnel management.

Every bank, large or small, commercial or cooperative, regional rural bank or development bank, old or newly established need to provide training to all employees, irrespective of their qualifications, skill and suitability for the job, at all times. Thus, no bank organisation can afford to deny the necessity to train its employees that too in ever changing socio-economic environment.

I. Meaning of Training

Once an employee is selected, placed and introduced, he or she must be provided with training in accordance with his job requirements. Training is the act of increasing the knowledge and skill of an employee for doing a particular job.

In other words, training moulds the employee's knowledge, skill, attitude, behaviour and aptitude towards the job and the requirements of the bank. It refers to the teaching activities carried on for the primary purpose of helping members of a bank to acquire and apply the knowledge which bridges the difference between job requirements and employees capabilities.

II. Need for Training in Bank

1. Matching talent with job : Whatever the past experience, qualification, skill or knowledge an employee may have, that may not exactly suit the job requirements of the bank. Thus every bank management finds deviations between employees present specifications and the job requirements so needed in the banks. Training is a tool through which such gap can be filled up by developing and moulding the employee's skill, knowledge, attitude, behaviour etc. in tune with the job requirements.

2. Productivity and profitability : Survival and progress of the bank depend upon its productivity and profitability. Training increases knowledge and skill of an employee which in turn help to improve the quantity and quality of work.

3. Technical advances : Every bank in order to improve and to be effective should adopt the latest technology that is likely to be mechanising, computerising and automating its working. To achieve this, bank should regularly train their employees to enrich them in the areas of technical advances.

4. Diversification and growth : For a sustainable growth, some diversification is a must which may bring a tremendous pressure of work on an employee. Training is necessary to enable the bank staff to get themselves familial' with the new approach, aid provides capabilities to face the changes in coordination with other staff of the bank.

5. Human relations : These days management of most of the banks has to maintain human relations besides maintaining sound industrial relations. So, the training in the field of human relations is very much necessary to deal with human problems and maintaining human relations,

6. Customer service: Job knowledge, specific skills and proper attitudinal orientation of bank staff is very important. An important reason for indifferent service to customers is inadequate job knowledge and lack of consciousness. Therefore, training programmes of banks should lay emphasis on customer service, courtesy, public relations, skills, telephone manners, grievance handling, etc. to achieve that Customer is a business'.

7. Banks stability and flexibility : Stability in any organisation goes with flexibility to face the environmental threats. In and out of staff is a continuous phenomenon therefore a reservoir of human talent must be created through training programmes to meet the loss of key personnel.

8. Other : Training is also necessary when the existing employee is promoted to a higher level in the bank and when there is some new job or occupation due to transfer. Training is also necessary to equip old employees with the advanced disciplines, techniques or technology.

III. Training Objectives in Banks

Keeping with the goals and objectives of the bank, the personnel manager, formulates the following training objectives:

1. To impart to new entrants the basic knowledge and skill they need for an intelligent performance of definite skill.
2. To prepare the employers, both new and old, to meet the present as well as changing requirements of the job and the bank.
3. To assist employees to function more effectively in their present positions by exposing them to the latest concepts, information and techniques.

4. To build up a second line of competent officers and prepare them to occupy more responsible positions.
5. To develop the potential of people for the next level job.
6. To ensure economical output of required quality.
7. To broaden the minds of senior managers by providing them with opportunities to share the experiences within and outside the bank.
8. To ensure smooth and efficient working of a bank, and
9. To promote individual and collective morale, a sense of responsibility, cooperative attitudes and good relationships among line staff.

IV. Areas of Training in Bank

In the following areas training is to be provided to an employee.

1. Bank policies and procedures : Training in this area is to be provided with a view to acquaint the new employees in respect to bank rules, practices, procedures, traditions, management, organisation structure, environment and services that are to be rendered to the clients.

2. Training in particular skills : Training in particular skills is given to enable the employees to become more effective on job. Training is given to employees regarding various skills necessary to carry out the actual job. For example, the clerk in a bank should be trained in the skills of making entries correctly in the ledger, skills of arithmetical calculations, quick comparison of figures and the like.

3. Human relations training : A human relations training assumes greater significance in banks as bank employees have to maintain human relations not only with other employees but also with their customers. Bank employees are to be trained in the areas of self learning, interpersonal competence and relations, treating the people as human beings rather than as machines, treating the people as human being as a social and psychological man rather than as an economic man. and the like. Thus, training enables the employees to achieve better team work, which leads to improved efficiency and productivity of the bank.

4. Managerial and supervisory training : Even non-managers sometimes perform managerial and supervisory functions like planning, decision-making, organising, maintaining inter personal relations, directing and controlling. Hence, management has to train the employees in managerial and supervisory skills.

V. Training Methods

The training methods commonly used to train employees in banks are as below:

1. On the job training : This is the most commonly used method which is also known as job instruction training. Under this method individual is placed on a regular job and taught the skills necessary to perform that job. The trainee learns under the guidance of a qualified instructor or senior employee. This method has the advantage of giving first hand knowledge and experience under actual working conditions. While the trainee is learning how to perform a job, he is also a regular worker rendering the services for which he is paid. The main forms on the job training are coaching, understudy and job rotation.

2. Off-the-job training : Under this method of training the trainee is separated from the job situation and his attention is focussed upon learning the material related to his future job performance. Since the trainee is not distracted by job requirements, he can place his entire concentration on learning the job rather than spending his time in performing it. Off the job training may be imparted in classroom or training institute or in a specially constructed building known as vestibule.

VI. Training Practices in Indian Banking

Since Nationalisation, commercial banks in India have grown in size and their operations have become diversified. Therefore adequate supply of well trained staff has become essential. Several training schemes and courses have been designed by national institute of bank management, Pune. as well as by the Indian institute of Bankers. Mumbai to develop functional and managerial skills among bank employees. A professional banker must have a sound knowledge and technical competence in the specialised field. New entrants must be inducted and groomed in the culture and philosophy of banking. A large and continuous supply of managerial staff has to be ensured to keep pace with the rapid geographic network of branches.

The following institutions have been providing training and developmental facilities to bank employees in India:

- The Indian Institute of Bankers. Murnbai.
- National Institute of Bank Management Pune.
- Training college of RBI.
- Training institutes of individual banks.

VII. Research Findings Related to Training Given in SBBJ and IDBI

Various aspects like kind of training given, training period, how training helped, what problems were faced and satisfaction of employees with training programs were studied in both the banks. The findings have been tabulated below.

1. Number of training programmes attended by respondent : The respondents of both the banks were asked questions regarding the number of training programmes attended by them. Training programmes helps the employees to improve the level of performance and to perform better by using better method of work and techniques. The research findings regarding number of training programme attended by respondents are as follows:

SBBJ

50% respondents attended 1-2 training programmes, 26% respondents attended 3-4 training programme, 14% attended 5-6 training programme while only 10% respondents attended more than six training programmes.

S.No.	Recognition Category	Respondent Bank			
		SBBJ	%	IDBI	%
1.	Nil	0	0	1	2
2.	One-Two	25	50	21	42
3.	Three-Four	13	26	16	32
4.	Five-Six	7	14	6	12
5.	More than six	5	10	6	12
	Total	**50**	**100**	**50**	**100**

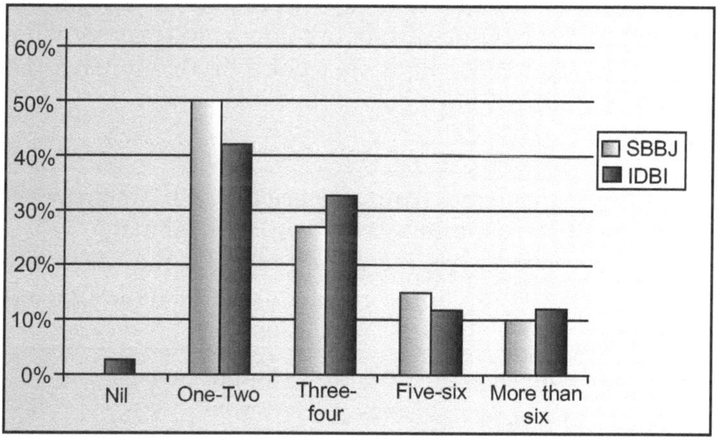

IDBI

Out of a total of 50 respondents, 42% respondents attended 1-2 training program. 32 and 12% respondents attended 3-4 and 5-6 training programmes respectively. 12% respondents attended more than 6 training programmes. Rest 2% respondents are those who did not attended any training programmes.

On analysis it is found that in both banks approximately 50% respondents attended 1-2 training programmes only. No major difference was seen regarding respondents attending 3-4, 5-6 and more than six training programmes in both the banks.

Chi Sq Test

To find out whether any significant difference exists between the two banks on the basis of number of training programmes attended by respondents in banks chi sq was conducted. The calculated value of chi sq was 1.78. The table value of chi sq for 4 d.f. at 5% level of significance is 9.488. Since the calculated value of chi sq is less than table value it indicates that there is no significant difference between the two banks on the basis of number of training programmes attended by respondents in two banks.

2. Period of training : The respondents of SBBJ and IDBI were asked questions related to their period of training. Period of training means how longer the candidates/respondents are being imparted training which can range from few days to weeks or to months. The responses obtained have been tabulated below:

SBBJ

For 50% of respondents training period was 1-3 months only while for 26% respondents it was 3-6 months. 14% of respondents had a training period of more than 6 months and only 10% said that their training period was upto 1 month only.

S.No.	Recognition Category	Respondent Bank			
		SBBJ	%	IDBI	%
1.	Up to 1 mth	5	10	4	8
2.	1-3 mth	25	50	21	42
3.	3-6 mth	13	26	16	32
4.	More than 6 mth	7	14	3	6
5.	Not Applicable	9	9	6	12
	Total	50	100%	50	100%

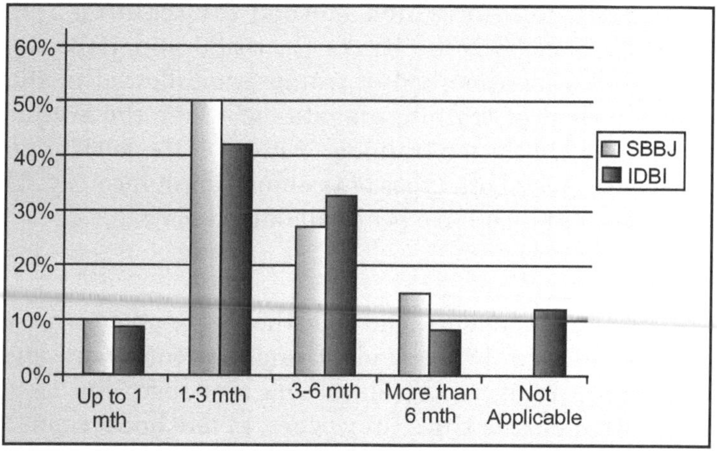

IDBI

42% of respondents were trained for 1-3 months while 32% were trained for 3-6 months. 6% of respondents were given training for a period of more than 6 months and 8% of the respondents were given training for period upto 1 month. Rest 12% of the respondents were not given training.

On analysis it was found that in both banks maximum number of respondents was given training for a period of 1-3 months only. It was found that SBBJ is giving training for long period to few employees in comparison to IDBI. 12% of the respondents were not given training in IDBI as there was no training period for them.

Chi Sq Test

To find out whether any significant difference exists between the two banks on the basis of period of training in batiks chi sq was conducted. The calculated value of chi sq was 5.37. The table value of chi sq for 4 d.f at 5% level of significance is 9.488, Since, the calculated value of chi sq is less than table value it indicates that there is no significant difference between the two banks on the basis of period of training of respondents.

3. Bank follows which method for training : The respondents of both the banks i.e. SBBJ and IDBI were asked that which method of training is followed in their bank. Method of training denotes whether the training imparted is 'On the job training' or it is 'Off the job training' or they are given both types of training simultaneously. The responses obtained have been tabulated below:

SBBJ

32% i.e. 16 respondents said that they were given training on work, 30% i.e. 15 respondent said that they were *given* separate training in the classroom and rest 38% i.e. 19 respondents said that they were given both types of training-on work and separate.

S.No.	Recognition Category	Respondent Bank			
		SBBJ	%	IDBI	%
1.	Training on work	16	32	19	38
2.	Separate Training	15	30	10	20
3.	Both	19	38	21	42
	Total	50	100	50	100

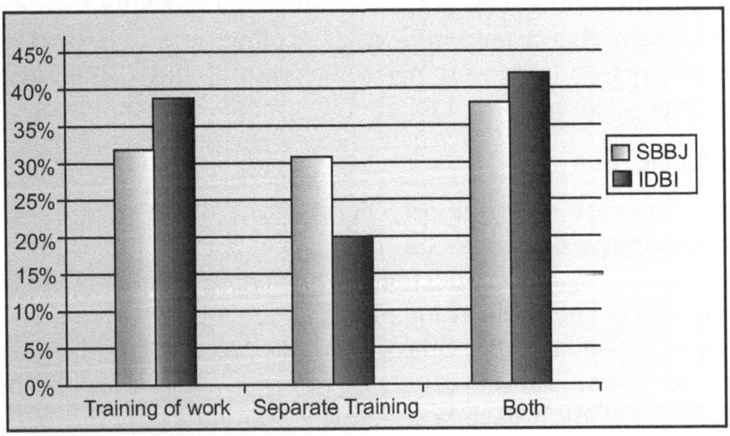

IDBI

38% i.e. 19 respondents said that they were given training on work, 20% i.e. 10 respondent said that they were given separate training in the classroom and rest 42% i.e. 21 respondents said that they were given both types of training-on work and separate.

On analysis it was found that in both the banks emphasis was more on both the types of training as it gives the respondent insight about on the job training also and separate training also. In IDBI the % of both types of training was more as compared to SBBJ.

Chi Sq Test

To find out whether any significant difference exists between the two banks on the basis of method of training in banks chi sq was conducted. The calculated value of chi sq was 1.36. The table value of chi sq for 2 d.f. at 5% level of significance is 5.991. Since, the calculated value of chi sq is less than table value it indicates that there is no significant difference between the two banks on the basis of method of training of respondents.

4. Extent of usefulness of training programme : The respondent's of both the banks were asked about their opinion regarding usefulness of training and how it helped them. The training programme helped the employees to grow in their career and develops new knowledge and skills among the employees which are a valuable asset to the organisation. It reduces employee's grievances as they are well trained personnel. The responses obtained have been tabulated below:

SBBJ

66% respondents said that training helped them in performing better on job, 18% said that training helped them in job satisfaction while rest 16% of respondent said that training helped them in promotion.

S.No.	Recognition Category	Respondent Bank			
		SBBJ	%	IDBI	%
1.	Better performance	33	66	31	62
2.	Job Satisfaction	9	18	10	20
3.	Promotion	8	16	9	18
	Total	50	100	50	100

IDBI

62% said that training helped them in better performance on job, 20% respondents said that training helped them in job satisfaction while rest 18% of respondents said that training helped them in promotion.

On analysis it was found that in both the banks maximum numbers of respondents were of the opinion that training helped them in performing better on job. In comparison to IDBI less number of respondents in SBBJ said that training helped them in job satisfaction. No major difference was seen in respondent's opinion regarding how training helped them in promotion.

Chi Sq Test

To find out whether any significant difference exists between the two banks on the basis of how training helped respondents in banks chi sq was conducted. The calculated value of chi sq was 0.17. The table value of chi sq for 2 d.f- at 5 % level of significance is 5.991. Since the calculated value of chi sq is less than table value it indicates that there is no significant difference between the two banks on the basis of how training helped the respondents.

5. Satisfaction with training programme : Training programme helps employees to be self reliant and motivated. It improved job satisfaction and morale, and helped the employee to grow further in the career. Respondent's opinion related to their extent of satisfaction with the training program is as below:

SBBJ

14% respondents said that they are to a great extent satisfied with training programme, 58% of the respondents were satisfied to an extent. 18% were satisfied to a little extent only, and rest 10% were not at all satisfied with the training programmes.

S.No.	Recognition Category	Respondent Bank			
		SBBJ	%	IDBI	%
1.	To a Great Extent	7	14	12	24
2.	To an extent	29	58	25	50
3.	To Little Extent	9	18	7	14
4.	Not at all	5	10	6	12
	Total	50		50	

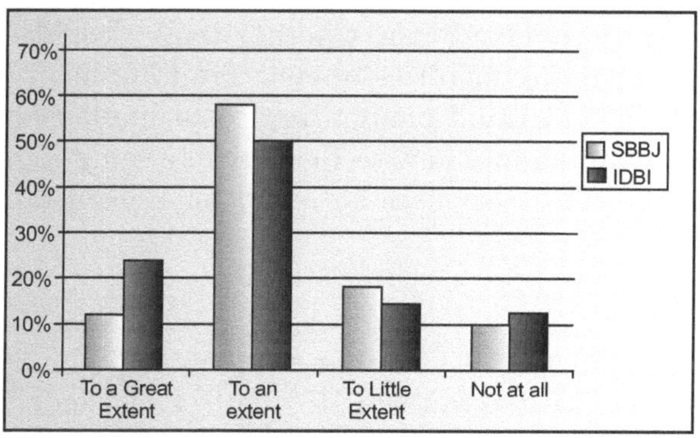

IDBI

Only 24% respondents were satisfied to a great extent 50% respondents were satisfied to an extent. 14% were satisfied to a little extent and rest 12% were not at all satisfied with the training programme.

To evaluate any programme satisfaction of beneficiaries is an important yardstick. It is observed that in both banks about 50% respondents were satisfied to some extent with the training programme. A major point to be noted is that very few respondents are satisfied to a great extent in both banks, although banks are spending huge amount on training of employees in both banks few respondents were not satisfied with the training programme.

Chi Sq Test

To find out whether any significant difference exists between the two banks on the basis of satisfaction of respondents with training programmes in banks chi sq was conducted. The calculated value of chi sq was 1.9530. The table value of chi sq for 3 d.f. at 5% level of significance is 7.815. Since the calculated value of chi sq is less than table value it indicates that there is no significant difference between the two banks on the basis of satisfaction of respondents "with training programmes in banks.

6. Providing adequate training facilities to employees : The respondents of both the banks i.e. SBBJ and IDBI were asked that whether bank provides them adequate training facilities or not. Training facilities are required due to rapid change in the technologies which requires training into new technology like computerisation in banking. The responses obtained have been tabulated below:

SBBJ

16% i.e. 8 respondents said that adequate training facilities are always provided to them, 48% i.e. 24 respondents said that training facilities are not always provided but are often provided to them, and rest 36% i.e. 18 respondents said that the bank had never provided adequate training facilities to them.

S.No.	Recognition Category	Respondent Bank			
		SBBJ	%	IDBI	%
1.	Always	8	16	11	22
2.	Often	24	48	30	60
3.	Never	18	36	9	18
	Total	**50**	**100**	**50**	**100**

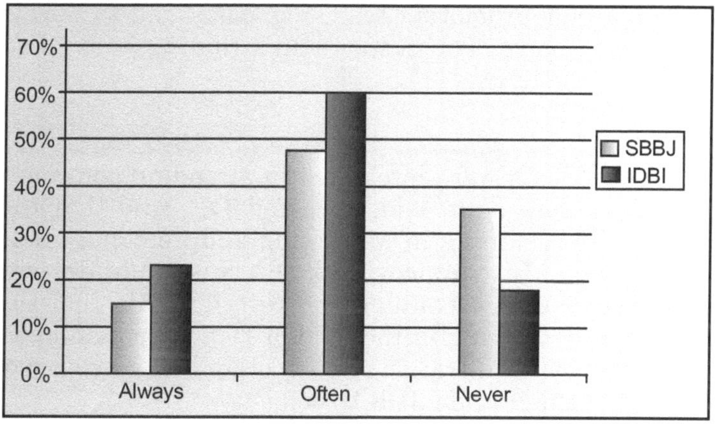

IDBI

2% i.e. 11 respondents said that adequate training facilities are always provided to them, 60% i.e. 54 respondents said that training facilities are not always provided but are often provided to them, and rest 18% i.e. 9 respondents said that the bank had never provided adequate training facilities to them.

On analysis it was found that in both the banks maximum respondents are of the view that often the bank provides adequate facilities to them.

Chi Sq Test

To find out whether any significant difference exists between the two banks on the basis of adequate training facilities provided, chi sq was conducted. The calculated value of chi sq was 4.14. The table value of chi sq for 2 d.f. at 5% level of significance is 5.991. Since the calculated value of chi sq is less than table value it indicates that there is no significant difference between the two banks on the basis of adequate training facilities provided to respondents.

7. Areas of training programme : The respondents were asked about the areas in which they would like to take training to improve their effectiveness. Trained employees can perform better and thereby earn more. Training helps the people for promotion to higher posts and to develop future managers. The respondent's findings have been tabulated as follows:

SBBJ

16% respondents were interested in attending training in general management field, 14% and 12% said that they want to take training in Marketing and Personnel fields respectively. In finance field 16% respondents were interested to attend training and rest 36% said that they want to take training in the field of IT and remaining 6% said that they want training in any other areas like Export Import Documentation, H.R.D. etc.

S.No.	Recognition Category	Respondent Bank			
		SBBJ	%	IDBI	%
1.	General Management	8	16	6	12
2.	Marketing	7	14	9	18
3.	Personnel	6	12	8	16
4.	Finance	8	16	12	24
5.	Information and Technology	18	36	13	26
6.	Any other Areas	3	6	2	4
	Total	50	100	50	100

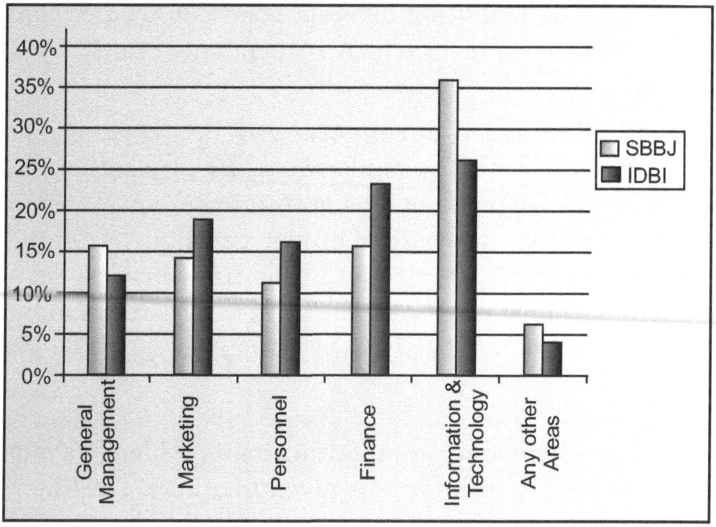

IDBI

12% and 18% respondents said that they would like to attend training in fields of General Management and Marketing respectively, 16% and 24% respondents wanted to attend training in field of personnel and finance respectively. Rest 26% said that they want to acquire training in IT field to improve their effectiveness and remaining 4% wants to attend training in any other areas like Export Import Documentation. H.R.D. etc.

On analysis it is observed that in both banks maximum number of respondents are interested in acquiring training in field of IT.

Chi Sq Test

To find out whether any significant difference exists between the two banks on the basis of area in which respondents want to take training chi sq was conducted. The calculated value of chi sq was 2.12. The table value of chi sq for 5 d.f. at 5% level of significance is 11.070. Since the calculated value of chi sq is less than table value it indicates that there is no significant difference between the two banks on the basis of area in which respondents want to take training.

8. Problem faced during training programme : The respondents of both the banks were asked whether they faced any kind of problem during training or not. Problems in training refer to whether proper training techniques, proper literature and adequate time have been spent by trainers in imparting training or not. The respondent's findings are tabulated as below:

SBBJ

12% i.e. 6 respondents faced favouritism problem, as much attention during training was given to others. 2294 i.e. 11 respondents faced the problem of poor guidance of the trainers, 10% i.e. 5 respondents are of the view that proper time was not there for training, and rest 56% i.e. 28 respondents said that they had not faced any problem.

S.No.	Recognition Category	Respondent Bank			
		SBBJ	%	IDBI	%
1.	Favouritism	6	12	11	22
2.	Poor Guidance	11	22	9	18
3.	Not given proper time	5	10	5	10
4.	No problem	28	56	25	50
	Total	50		50	

IDBI

22% i.e. 11 respondents faced favouritism problem, as much attention during training was given to others, 18% i.e. 9 respondents faced the problem of poor guidance of the trainers. 10% i.e. 5 respondents are of the view that proper time was not there for training, and rest 50% i.e. 25 respondents said that they had not faced any problem.

On analysis it was observed that in both the banks maximum number of respondents did not faced any problem during training. Problem of favouritism was seen more in IDBI in comparison to SBBJ. Regarding problem of not given proper time and poor guidance similar views were obtained from respondents of both banks.

Chi Sq Test

To find out whether any significant difference exists between the two banks on the basis of problems faced by respondents during training chi sq was conducted. The calculated value of chi sq was 1.84. The table value of chi sq for 3 d.f. at 5% level of significance is 7.815. Since the calculated value of chi sq is less than table value it indicates that there is no significant difference between the two banks on the basis of problems faced by respondents during training.

REFERENCES

Chaterjii N.M. : Management of Personnel in Indian Enterprises, Allied Book Agency, Calcutta.

Desai Vasant : Principles of Bank Management, Himalaya Publishing House, Mumbai.

Gupta C.B. : Principles of Management for Banker's, Sultan Chand & Sons, New Delhi.

Subbaro P : Principles and Practice of Bank Management, Himalaya Publishing House, New Delhi.

Subramaniam C.V. : Human Resource Management, Sultan Chand & Co., New Delhi.

CHAPTER

11

Human Resource Development in Cement Industries

Prof. Basant Mehta
Dr. Hemant Sumani

Cement industry is one of the core industries of the country, like iron and steel industry. It is the main pillar of any economy. It plays very vital role in the development of the country.

Human Resource Development

Human Resource Development in cement industries is a countrywide issue and the subject of human resource development is everlasting value. It has unending facets and one can not say with certainty as to what ideal theme of developing of human resource. But inspite of this human resource is a very momentous part of our Organizations and development of human resource is main thing to progress of the Organizations. It is the most significant and active factor of production, become the key to optimize the utilization of all the other material resources. Developing the human resources, upgrading their skill and knowledge would lead to economic and organizational development. To take full advantage of development of human participation with increased efficiency and skill is very essential.

Analysis of Field Work

The data for this investigation were collected from primary as well as secondary sources, For collection of primary data the following two types of schedules were constructed and adopted.

(*a*) Schedule for employee of cement industries.

(*b*) Schedule for management of cement industries.

The first schedule has been prepared to collect information relating to the employees of different categories (i.e. officer, clerical, labour) in Birla Cement Works, J.K. Cement Works and Aditya Cement. The second schedule was used to collect information relating to managers of Birla Cement Works, J.K. Cement Works and Aditya Cement.

For the first schedule, 25 employees were selected at random from each categories (i.e. officer, clerical, labour) working in selected cement industries, Hence 75 employees were selected from Birla Cement Works, J.K. Cement Works and Aditya Cement, so in all 225 employees were selected for this study. While for second schedule 10 managers were selected at random from Birla Cement Works, J.K. Cement Works and Aditya Cement, so in all 30 managers were selected for this study.

Main Findings of the Study

On the basis of the observation and analysis of various aspects of human resource development in Birla Cement Works, J.K. Cement Works and Aditya Cement, the researcher has reached on the conclusion that on the whole human resource development in nice way.

- There is no existence of H.R.D. department in J.K. Cement Works and personnel department perform H.R.D. functions. While in Birla Cement Works and Aditya Cement H.R.D. department perform recruitment, selection, placement, career planning, training programme, feedback and counselling etc.
- In Birla Cement Works and J.K. Cement Works generally training period was 3-6 months for new employees while in Aditya Cement training period was only one month, about 4/5 employees and most of the

mangers of the three cement units confess that organization follows both (Training on work and Separate Training) method for training. More than 90 per cent employees and about all the managers of the three cement units observed that training help to employees for better performance.

- In the selected three units nearly 90 per cent employees were satisfied with their salary. In Aditya Cement all the employees received bonus however in Birla Cement Works and J.K. Cement Works about 1/3 employees received bonus and nearly 1/3 employees of three units received overtime. About the cent per cent employees of Birla Cement Works, J.K. Cement Works and Aditya Cement received Medical, L.T.C. and Vehicle/Petrol allowance but in Aditya Cement uniform allowance is also provided and these allowances paid on fixed basis.
- The survey reveals that all the cement units provide medical facilities to their employees and family members. In these medical facilities Birla Cement Works and Aditya Cement provide treatment in their hospital, case reimbursement for outside treatment. While mediclaim insurance is provided in Birla Cement Works and J.K. Cement Works to only staff employees, not for workers.
- The study indicates that most of the employees and managers of three cement units stated that fire extinguisher, fire pump and smoke deductor are available and helmet, shoes, torch, gloves, glasses safety belts for height are provided to employees according to their job nature. While more than 90 per cent employees and cent per cent managers of three cement units admitted that training given to employees about safety measures and they are satisfied with safety measures. Employees and manager of three cement units admitted that hospital

facility, monetary facilities for treatment, leave with salary and compensation are provided in case of accidents.

- The research shows that 2/5 employees of three cement units agreed that generally management encourage to employees with new methods and ideas and appreciate for contribution of increasing productivity while all the managers stated most of the times organizations encourage to employees for applying new methods and creative ideas and appreciate to employees for contribution for increasing productivity.
- Managers and employees of three cement units believes that monetary and non-monetary both incentive plan are available for employees encouragement.
- Management of three cement units motivate to employees with giving rewards, monetary benefits, promotion and encourage to employees in time to time for increasing productivity.
- The survey shows that nearly all the employees of three cement units were promoted and they promoted on seniority and on merit basis and in the opinion of all the managers of three cement units employees are promoted on due time and they promoted on seniority and on merit basis.
- All the managers and employees of three cement units reported that employee rarely demoted and reason for demotion was improper working and misbehave with management.
- The survey clearly indicates that in the three cement units the management and the employees relation was quite good, harmonious and friendly and most of the employees and managers reported that they never faced dispute with each other.

- The survey indicates that 40 per cent employees of Birla Cement Works, nearly 60 per cent employees of J.K. Cement Works and 68 per cent employees of Aditya Cement were not aware about the career development plan. While more than 70 per cent employees of the three selected cement units feel that management is normally sympathetic with their problems and normally consider employees qualification and expertise while making salary, allowances and perquisites.
- Most of the employees feel that their salary was adequate according to their job work and most of the employees were satisfied with their working condition and job opportunities.
- The investigation indicates that Provident Fund and Gratuity benefits are available to all employees in the three cement units. Superannuation benefits is available only for staff employees in Birla Cement Works and J.K. Cement Works and in Aditya Cement it is applicable for senior officers, while managers of three cement units reported that organization provide Provident Fund, Gratuity benefits and Superannuation benefits to employees at the time of retirement and 2/5 managers of Birla Cement Works and J.K. Cement Works reported that pension benefits is also provided to employees at the time of retirement.

Testing of Hypothesis

1. The result of this investigation proves our hypothesis:

   "In cement industries proper social securities facilities were provided by management to their workers".

   The basis of this conclusion mentioned below:

   Cent per cent employees in Birla Cement Works, J.K. Cement Works and Aditya Cement got Provident Fund and Gratuity benefits at the time of retirement while 64 per cent, 67 per cent and 5 per cent employees in Birla Cement Works, J.K. Cement Works and Aditya Cement Works, J.K. Cement Works and Aditya Cement respectively received superannuation benefits. 25 per cent employees in Birla Cement Works and 24 per cent in J.K. Cement Work got pension benefits.

2. The result of this investigation clearly disapproves the hypothesis of the study that "In cement industries worker's had many grievances and disputes with management".

   This conclusion has been arrived on the basis of following findings:

   99 per cent employees in Birla Cement Works and cent per cent employees of J.K. Cement Works and Aditya Cement have harmonious and friendly relation with management and 80 per cent, 61 per cent and 75 per cent employees of Birla Cement Works, J.K. Cement Works and Aditya Cement respectively never faced disputes with management and cent per cent employees of selected units reported that in last 5 years no lockout or strike take place in the organizations.

REFERENCES

Books

Bhatia, B.S. and Batra G.S. : Encyclopaedia of Business Management, Deep and Deep Publications, New Delhi, 1999.

Bhatia, B.S. and Verma, H.L. : Studies in Human Resource Development, Deep and Deep Publications, New Delhi, 1996.

Holloran, Jack : Personnel and Human Resource Management, Prentice Hall, Englewood Cliffs, NJ, 1986.

Jayagopal, R. : Human Resource Development Conceptual Analysis and Strategies, Sterling Publishers Private Limited, New Delhi, 1990.

Khandelwal, Anil K. : Human Resource Development, Oxford and IBH Publishing Co., New Delhi, 1996.

Kohli, Uddesh and Sinha, Dharni : Human Resource Development in 2000 AD, IJTD, New Delhi.

Kohli, Uddesh and Vinayshil, Gotam : HRD—Global Changes Strategies and Planning Process in India, IJTD, New Delhi.

Laxminaraian, M.L. : Worker's Participation in Public Enterprises, Himalaya Publishing House, Bombay, 1986.

Mehta, Basant and Kothari, Kiran : Human Resource Development (Vol. 1, 2), Discovery Publishing House, New Delhi, 1999.

Parda, Jayant Kumar and Jena Rana Kanta : HRD-Concept and Mechanism in Management of Human Assets, M.G. Rao, Discovery Publishing House, New Delhi, 1993.

Pareek, Udai and Rao, T.V. : Designing and Managing Human Resource Systems, Oxford & IBM, New Delhi, 1981.

Rao, T.V. : HRD Practices in Indian Industry, Indian Institute of Management, Ahmedabad, 1981.

Saiyadin, Mirza S. : Human Resource Management, Tata McGraw Hill Publishing Co., New Delhi, 1988.

Articles

Grant, N.B. : Management Development and All the Public Sector Concept, Lok Udhyog, Vol. IX, No. 6, Sept-1995.

Gupta, C.B. : Human Resource Management in Public Enterprises, Jodhpur Management Journal, Vol. 1, 1983-84.

Khan, Irshad H. : Management Training.and Development in Public Enterprises, IPE Journal.

Mehta, Basant : Human Resource Development under PMRY, The Indian Journal of

		Commerce, Vol. No. 191, Part-11, June 1997.
Minocha, O.P.	:	Training in Public Sector Undertakings : A Systematic Approach, Indian Journal of Public Administration, Vol. 34, No. 3 (July-Sept.) 1998.
Nodler, Len	:	Defining the Field—It is IIRD or OD, Training and Development Journal, Vol. 34, No. 2, pp. 66-68.
Rangnekar, Sharu S.	:	Changing Pattern of Human Resource Development, Indian Journal of Training and Development 8(4), July - August 1978.
Ravi Shanker, S. and Mishra, R.K.	:	Management Development and Training in Public Enterprises, Institute of Public Enterprises Journal, Hyderabad, Dec. 1981.

Cement Industries Publications

- Annual Reports of Birla Corporation Limited
- Annual Reports of J.K. Organization
- Annual Reports of Grasim Industries Ltd
- Basic Data, Indian Cement Industry
- Executive Summary, Cement Industry
- Cement Statistics
- Indian Cement Industry, Statistics

SECTION–III
FINANCIAL MANAGEMENT

CHAPTER

12

A Study of Deposit Services Provided by Public and Private Sector Banks (Analysis of Gap in Service Quality through SERVQUAL)

Prof. Basant Mehta
Miss Kiran Vazirani

Introduction

The reason why companies offer quality is to satisfy the customer (Dale, 1999). A key aspect in customer satisfaction is the way a customer can get satisfies or dissatisfies with a company's service. If a company wants to satisfy its customers, the first problem is that ist need to know—what it is that satisfies customers and equally important, what it is that makes customers dissatisfied with the company, its products and services. Whether customers are satisfied or not, depends on the balance between customers' expectations and customers' experiences with the products and services (Zeithaml et al., 1990). When a company is able to lift a customer's experience to a level that exceeds that customers' expectation, then that customer will be satisfied. Thus, in recent periods, customer satisfaction from service providers' perspective got significant research interests. Ample of study results depict different ways to serve the customers leading to satisfaction. Parasuraman et al., (1985, 1988) advocated such tool where service quality gap is calculated to find out the areas where there is a gap in satisfaction and named it as SERVQUAL.

In Udaipur city, banking industry is highly explored by research community. Still, studies on customer satisfaction from a banker's perspective are rare. And depositors are not only the customers; they are also the owners as they provide money on which banks operate. Thus, keeping the depositors satisfied is highly demanded in banking industry though it is sometimes overlooked as we find in Udaipur city. The current research targets to calculate the gap scores using SERVQUAL scale that will ultimately conclude the reasons for dissatisfaction of depositors with the bank. It will also bear an important message for the bankers as to what it should do for keeping its depositors satisfies. The next section contains a detailed introduction of SERVQUAL scale and gap. Later on, the current research methodology is presented with detailed analysis, design and findings of the study. Finally the discussion is ended with conclusion and recommendations.

The SERVQUAL Scale and the Gap

The SERVQUAL approach to the measurement of service quality has attracted considerable attention since first introduced by Parasuraman et al. in 1985. In the early 1980's, Parasuraman, Zeithaml and Berry conducted an extensive programme of qualitative research with business people and consumers to explore the concept of service quality. They concluded that service quality as perceived by customers depends on the gap between their expectations and the level of service that was actually provided.

They also initially identified ten components of service quality, including constructs such as competence, courtesy, credibility and security. This list was later reduced to five constructs—tangibles, responsiveness, empathy, assurance and reliability when they have extended their research in 1988 forming the basis of a scale called SERVQUAL

(Parasuraman, Zeithaml and Berry, 1988) with the perspective meanings as given below:

(*a*) **Tangibles** : the appearance of the physical facilities and materials related to the service

(*b*) **Reliability** : the ability to perform the service accurately and dependably

(*c*) **Responsiveness** : The willingness to help customers and provide prompt service

(*d*) **Assurance** : The competence of the system and its security, credibility and courtesy.

(*e*) **Empathy** : the ease of access, approachability and effort taken to understand customer's requirement.

Research Objectives and Research Methodology

The broad purpose of this paper is to analyze the gaps between expectation and perception of deposit services provided by a Govt. Bank and a Private Bank; their identities are intentionally hidden to make the study technically viable. The rationale of selecting the industry and area is well founded. It has already been seen that there is a huge gap between the service delivery by a Govt. Bank and a Private Bank. Govt. Banks have good amount of market share, with lowest service charges. But still Private Banks enjoy a good market share majorly because of good services, better approach, etc. So the researcher got interested to work in this area to identify the level of satisfaction amongst both the types of banks. SERVQUAL is widely recognized and accepted, and it is regarded as applicable to a number of industries as stated above, including banking industry (Yavas, Bilgin, Shemuell, 1997)

Population and Sample

It is a comparison of the status of service quality across two different banks. So the depositors of both of these banks are the population for the research. Through random sampling, researcher has taken a sample of 125 respondents for each of these banks. During the data entry, 12 questionnaires of Govt. Bank and 9 questionnaires of Private Bank had been rejected due to incomplete filling and for reducing response biasedness.

Administration of Questionnaire

The genetic questionnaire as used by Parasuraman et al. (1988) has been used here with 22 statements under 5 dimensions. The responses have been captured in 7-point Likert Scale and gap score is calculated by deducting expectations from perceptions (E - P). At the time of collecting data, proper care has been given to the demographic profile of the users to ensure that the result is free from any sort of biasness.

Data Collection, Analysis and Findings

The use of SERVQUAL is analyzed here in greater detail with logical sequences. It starts with all of the 22 original statements categorized into five in the form of a questionnaire and a 7-point scale is used to collect the customer's expectations and perceptions. The difference between these expectations (E) and perceptions (P) is the gap score which is then averaged (both weighted and un-weighted). Simple descriptive statistics are used for data analysis. The methodology is presented below stepwise:

Step 1 : Designing SERVQUAL Instrument

Designing SERVQUAL instrument is very much important as data will be captures through this. The simple way of doing it is adopting the original instrument as designed by Parasuraman et al. (1988) with 22 statements in 5 categories. In this study the researcher has used the original instrument as given below in detail. The same instrument has been provided to the respondents of both the banks.

Table 12.1. Expectations and Perception Analysis of a Govt. Bank and a Private bank

Strongly Disagree Expectations Tangibles	Strongly Agree						
	E (Govt.)	E (Pvt.)	Perceptions Tangibles	P (Govt.)	P (Pvt.)	Gap Score E-P (Govt.)	Gap Score E-P (Pvt.)
1	2	3	4	5	6	7	8
E-1. Excellent banking companies will have modern looking equipment.	5.7	6.2	P-I. Your Bank has modern looking equipment	3.1	6.0		
						2.6	0.2
E-2. The physical facilities at excellent banks will be visually appealing.	6.2	6.0	P - 2. Your Bank's physical . facilities are visually appealing	2.9	5.8		
						3.3	0.2
E - 3. Employees at excellent banks will be well dressed and appear neat.	6.5	6.2	P-3. Your Bank's employees are well dressed and appear neat.	2.8	6.0		
						3.7	0.2
E -4. Materials associated with the service (statements) will be visually appealing at an excellent banks	5.2	6.3	P-4. Material associated with the service (such as statements) are visually appealing at Your Bank.	3.3	6.2		
						1.9	0.1
Total	**23.6**	**24.7**		**12.1**	**24**	**11.5**	**0.7**
Average Gap Score [Totalof E-P/4]						**2.875**	**0.175**

...(Contd.)

1	2	3	4	5	6	7	8
E-5. When excellent banks promise to do something by a certain time, they do.	6.3	6.0	P - 5. When Your Bank promises to do something by a certain time, it does so.	2.5	4.8		
						3.8	1.2
E-6. When a customer has a problem, excellent banks will show a sincere interest in solving it.	5.9	5.7	P-6. When you have a problem, Your Bank shows a sincere interest in solving it.	3.7	5.0		
						2.2	0.7
E-7. Excellent banks will perform the service right the first time.	5.8	5.7	P-7. Your Bank provides its service right the first time.	4.3	5.2		
						1.5	0.5
E-8. Excellent banks will provide the service at the time they promise to do so.	6.2	5.8	P-8. Your Bank provides its service at the time it promises to do	3.5	4.8		
						2.7	1.0
E- 9. Excellent banks will insist on error free records.	6.7	6.3	P-9. Your Bank insists on error free records.	4.2	5.8		
						2.5	0.5
Total	**30.9**	**29.5**		**18.2**	**25.6**	**12.7**	**3.9**
Average Gap Score [Total of E - P/4]						**2.54**	**0.78**

...(Contd.)

1	2	3	4	5	6	7	8
E-10. Employees of excellent banks will tell customers exactly when services will be performed.	5.8	5.5	P-10. Employees in Your Bank tell you exactly when services will be performed.	3.4	5.2		
						2.4	0.3
E-11. Employees of excellent banks will give prompt service to customers.	6.5	5.7	P-11. Employees in Your Bank give you prompt service.	2.5	4.8		
						4.0	1.1
E-12. Employees of excellent banks will always be willing to help customers.	6.8	5.8	P-12. Employees in Your Bank are always willing to help you.	2.8	4.8		
						4.0	1.0
E-13. Employees of excellent banks will never be too busy to respond to customer's requests.	5.6	5.5	P-13. Employees in Your Bank are never too busy to respond to your queries.	1.5	4.6		
						4.1	1.2
Total	**24.7**	**22.5**		**10.2**	**19.2**	**14.5**	**3.3**
Average Gap Score [Total of E - P/]						**3.625**	**0.825**

...(Contd.)

1	2	3	4	5	6	7	8
E-14. The behavior of employees in excellent banks will instill confidence in customers	5.7	6.3	P-14. The behavior of employees in Your Bank instills confidence in you.	40	5.5		
						1.7	0.8
E-15. Customers of excellent banks will feel safe in transaction	6.3	6.2	P-1 5 . You feel safe in your transactions with Your Bank	5.5	5.7		
						0.8	0.5
E-16. Employees of excellent banks will feel consistently courteous with customers.	6.0	5.7	P-16. Employees in Your Bank are consistently courteous with you.	3.1	5.1		
						2.9	0.6
E-17. Employees of excellent banks will have the knowledge to answer customer's questions	6.3	6.0	P-17. Employees in Your Bank have the knowledge to answer your questions.	3.5	5.5	2.8	0.5
Total	**24.3**	**24.2**		**16.1**	**21.8**	**8.2**	**2.4**
Average Gap Score [Total of E-P/]						**2.05**	**0.6**

...(Contd.)

1	2	3	4	5	6	7	8
E-18. Excellent banks will give customers individual attention.	6.1	5.5	P-18. Your Bank gives you individual attention.	2.6	4.3		
						3.5	1.2
E-19. Excellent banks will have operating hours convenient to all their customers.	5.8	5.8	P-19. Your Bank has operating hours convenient to all its customers.	4.9	5.6		
						0.9	0.2
E-20. Excellent banks will be having employees who give customers personal attentions.	6.2	5.7	P-20. Your Bank has employees who give you personal attention.	2.5	4.2		
						3.7	1.5
E-21. Excellent banks will have their customer's best interests at heart.	5.4	5.5	P-21. Your Bank has your best interest at heart.	2.2	4.2		
						3.2	1.3

...(Contd.)

1	2	3	4	5	6	7	8
E-22. The employees of excellent banks will understand the specific needs of their customers.	6.4	5.3	P-22. The employees of Your Bank understand your specific needs.	3.3	4.2		
						3.1	1.3
Total	**29.9**	**27.8**		**15.5**	**22.3**	**14.4**	**5.5**
Average Gap Score (E-P/ 4]						**2.88**	**1.1**

Respondents are advised to put a value between 1 and 7 against each statement twice; one for expectations and another for perceptions. Then the gap score is calculated and averaged as given above. Following table shows the expectation and perception gap of services provided by a Private bank.

Step 2 : Calculation of Un-weighted Score

Gap scores for five different categories as calculated in step 1 for both the banks is averaged to compute un-weighted average score as given below:

Table 12.2. Average Scores of each Dimension for a Govt. Bank and a Multinational Bank

Sl. No.	Categories	Gap Scores for Govt. Bank	Gap Scores for Private Bank
1.	Average score for Tangibles	2.875	0.175
2.	Average score for Reliability	2.54	0.78
3.	Average score for Responsiveness	3.625	0.9
4.	Average score for Assurance	2.05	0.6
5.	Average score for Empathy	2.88	1.1
	Total	13.97	3.555
	Average (Total/5) Un-Weighted	2.794	0.8875

Step 3 : Assigning Weights

This step is the extension of the SERVQUAL score and is only required if weighted score is calculated. Putting weights against each of the five dimensions is critical and tactful because.

Table 12.3. Weights assigned for each dimensions of both the Banks

Sl. No.	Dimensions	Points by Govt. Bank Customers	Points by Private Bank Customers
1.	The appearance of banks physical facilities, equipment, personnel and communication material (Tangibles)	7	17
2.	The bank's ability to perform the promised service dependably and accurately (Reliability)	33	21
3.	The bank's willingness to help customers and provide prompt service (Responsiveness)	20	24
4.	The knowledge and courtesy of the bank's employees and their ability to convey trust and confidence (Assurance)	26	20
5.	The caring, individual attention they provide to its customers (Empathy)	14	18
	Total	100	100

The amount of weights represents the relative importance of the dimensions to the customer. The questionnaire has separate page asking each respondent to put relative weight against each dimensions. The points against each of the dimensions are totalled and averaged to normalize it. Total 100 points has been allocated and among these, five dimensions as stated below have been calculated considering respondent's point of view.

Step 4 : Calculation of Weighted Score

Step 2 and Step 3 will give us weighted score that comes through the calculation as stated below:

Table 12.4. Calculation of Weighted Score for both the Banks

Sl. No.	Dimensions	Govt. Bank			Private Bank		
		Un-weighted Score (Step 2)	Weights (Step 3)	Weighted Score	Un-Weighted Score (Step 2)	Weights (Step 3)	Weighted Score
1.	Tangibles	2.875	0.07	0.20125	0.175	0.17	0.0295
2.	Reliability	2.54	0.33	0.8382	0.78	0.21	0.1638
3.	Responsiveness	3.625	0.20	0.725	0.9	0.24	0.216
4.	Assurance	2.05	0.26	0.533	0.6	0.20	0.12
5.	Empathy	2.88	0.14	0.4032	1.1	0.18	0.198
	Total Weighted Score			**2.70065**			**0.7273**

Step 5 : Analyze and take Necessary Actions

Finally, the score should be analyzed to find out the weak areas where more attention is required. The gap score indicated the extent of gap in service quality. The larger the gap score is, the more is the dissatisfaction. Overall score under each category and total can be presented in a single table to get an overall picture as shown below:

Table 12.5. Summarize Gap analysis of a Govt. Bank

Sl. No.	Dimensions	Expectations (E)	Perceptions	Total Gap Sectors (E-P)	Average Gap Score	Weightings (W)	Weighted Score
1	Tangibles	23.6	12.1	11.5	2.875	0.07	0.20125
2	Reliability	30.9	18.2	12.7	2.54	0.33	0.8382
3	Responsiveness	24.7	10.2	14.5	3.625	0.20	0.725
4	Assurance	24.3	16.1	8.2	2.05	0.26	0.533
5	Empathy	29.9	15.5	14.4	2.88	0.14	0.4032
	Total						**2.70065**

Table 12.6. Summarize Gap analysis of a Private Bank

Sl. No.	Dimensions	Expectations (E)	Perceptions	Total Gap Sectors (E-P)	Average Gap Score	Weightings (E)	Weighted Score
1.	Tangibles	24.7	24.0	0.7	0.175	0.17	0.0295
2.	Reliability	29.5	25.6	3.9	0.78	0.21	0.1638
3.	Responsiveness	22.5	19.5	3.6	0.9	0.24	0.216
4.	Assurance	24.2	21.8	2.4	0.6	0.20	0.12
5.	Empathy	27.8	22.5	5.5	1.1	0.18	0.198
	Total						**0.7273**

The whole picture is clear now. The customers of Private bank are much more satisfied as compared to that of Govt. bank, as their Total Weighted Average Score is higher than that of Govt. bank. In Govt. bank, the dimension Responsiveness has the highest gap score (un-weighted). But after the adjustment with weights, the score becomes 0.725 that is no more the highest. But in case of Private Bank, the Empathy dimension has the highest gap score, but after adjustments with weights, it lost the first position and come to second position. Thus the weight has a lot of implication. Individually, the customers are very much dissatisfied in this category. But they believe that it should have less weight at the time of calculating aggregated score. On the basis of weighted score, the dimension Reliability (in Govt. bank) and Responsiveness (in Private bank) got the highest score. It means that the performance of the banks in these categories is not good and they should give sufficient attention to all of the sub-categories under this dimension.

Conclusion

Superior service quality is widely acknowledged as a driver of perceived value, which in turn, will enhance customer loyalty (Parasuraman and Grewal, 2000) and improve the provider's image, sales and profitability (Buzzell and Gale, 1987; Gummesson, 1993). Thus, the service provider should ensure superior service quality to bag customer loyalty. The study of customer satisfaction on a regular basis and taking steps to ensure more satisfaction should be a regular practice.

Use of SERVQUAL in banks is not uncommon. Here, it has been used for analyzing service quality of different banks in terms of deposit services provided by the banks. Such analysis is helpful in identifying the weak areas where immediate action is warranted. For example, the current study concludes that the customers of Govt. Bank are not satisfied in terms of "Reliability" and of Private Bank; customers had a bad experience in terms of "Responsiveness". Not only this, customers of Private bank are more satisfied with service quality gap as compared to that of customers of a Govt. bank. The score value individually may mean nothing; still it may reflect the ranking (thrusts areas) and improvements as compared with earlier years or periods. Finally, the dimensions used here may be replicated to customize it with typical nature of services under considerations.

REFERENCES

1. Abdullah, F., (2006). Measuring Service Quality in Higher Education: Hedperf *versus* SERVPERF, *Marketing Intelligence and Planning,* Vol. 24, No. 1, pp. 31-47.
2. Angur, M., Nataraajan, R., and Jahera, J., (1999). Service Quality in Banking Industry; An Assessment in a Developing Country, *International Journal of Bank Marketing,* Vol. 17, No. 3, pp. 116-123.
3. Babakus, E., and Mangold, W., (1989). Adapting the SERVQUAL Scale to Hospital Service: An Empirical Investigation, *Health Services Research,* Vol. 26, No. 6, pp. 62-81.
4. Cronin, J. J., Jr. and Taylor, S. A., (1992). Measuring Service Quality: A Reexamination and Extension. *Journal of Retailing,* Vol. 66, pp. 33-55.
5. Boulding, W., Kalra, A., Staelin, R., & Zeithaml, V. A. (1993). A Dynamic Process Model of Service Quality: From Expectations

to Behavioural Intentions. *Journal of Marketing Research,* 30(1), 7-27.

6. Brown, T., Churchill, G., and Peter, J., (1993). Improving the Measurement of Service Quality, *Journal of Retailing,* Vol. 69, No. 1, pp. 127-139.
7. Karatape, M. Osman, Yavas, Ugur., and Babakus Emin. (2005). Measuring Service Quality of Banks: Scale Development and Validation. *Journal of Retailing and Consumer Service,* Vol. 12, pp. 373-383.
8. Carman, J., (1990). Consumer Perceptions of Sendee Quality; An Assessment of SERVQUAL dimensions, *Journal of Retailing,* Vol. 66, pp. 33-35.
9. Shil, Chandra NikhiL, and Das, Dr. Bhagaban, (June, 2009) Analysis of Gap in Service Quality through SERVQUAL: A Case of Deposit Service Provided by a Bank in Bangladesh. *Indian Journal of Marketing,* pp. 3-11.

CHAPTER

13

International Financial Management

Global Meltdown and Its Impact on the Indian Economy

Prof. Basant Mehta
Miss Meghashree Agarwal

ABSTRACT

In the globalized market scenario, the impact of recession at one place/industry/sector peculate down to all the linked industry and this can be truly interpreted from the current market situation which is faced by the world. The badly hit sector at present is being the financial sector, and major issue being the *"LIQUIDITY Crises"* in the market. In present situation down fall in one sector one day leads to a negative impact on the other sector thus altogether everyone feel the impact of the Financial crises with the result of the current recession which started in US and slowly and gradually due to linked global world have impacted everyone. The government advised the sectors of weakening demand to reduce prices. It provided some relief by cutting down excise duties, but such simplistic solutions were doomed to failure.

The term *financial crisis* is applied broadly to a variety of situations in which some financial institutions or assets suddenly lose a large part of their value. In the 19th and early 20th centuries, many financial crises were associated with banking panics and many recessions coincided with these panics. Other situations that are often called financial crises include stock market crashes and the bursting of other financial bubbles, currency crises and sovereign defaults.

Keywords: *Finance-Financing, International finance, International Finance-Prominent Institutes, International Finance-Benefits, Finance in India, Financial Crisis, Global Meltdown and its Impact on the Indian Economy.*

Finance- Financing

Finance is a branch of economics that deals with the management of funds, financial resources and other assets. In broader terms, finance is raising or investing money either as equity or debt. Finance is a wide-ranging term which includes funding, investments, trading and risk management. *Finance* is the science of funds management. The general areas of finance are *business finance, personal finance,* and *public finance.* Finance includes saving money and often includes lending money. The field of finance deals with the concepts of time, money and risk and how they are interrelated. It also deals with how money is spent and budgeted. An entity whose income exceeds their expenditure can lend or invest the excess income. On the other hand, an entity whose income is less than its expenditure can raise capital by borrowing or selling equity claims, decreasing its expenses, or increasing its income. The lender can find a borrower, a financial intermediary such as a bank, or buy notes or bonds in the bond market. The lender receives interest, the borrower pays a higher interest than the lender receives, and the financial intermediary pockets the difference.

A specific example of corporate finance is the sale of stock by a company to institutional investors like investment banks, who in turn generally sell it to the public. The stock gives whoever owns it part ownership in that company. If you buy one share of XYZ Inc, and they have 100 shares outstanding (held by investors), you are 1/100 owner of that company. Of course, in return for the stock, the company receives cash, which it uses to expand its business; this process is known as "equity financing". Finance is used by individuals (personal finance), by governments (public finance), by businesses (corporate finance) as well as by a wide variety of organizations including schools and non-profit organizations. Finance is one of the most important aspects of business management. Without proper financial planning a new enterprise is unlikely to be successful. Managing money (a liquid asset) is essential to ensure a secure future, both for the individual and an organization.

International Finance

International finance, an offshoot of economics, encompasses a detailed understanding of exchange rates and foreign investment and their impact on international trade. Analysis of international projects, overseas investments, cross border capital flows, trade deficits, currency swaps and global financial markets are some of its key areas of study. Individual investors usually focus on that part of international finance that deals with global futures and options and the forex market. *International Finance* is concerned with the same methodology of allocating financial resources, but with modifications or areas of emphasis required by the restrictions of currency and capital movements among countries and the differences in the currencies used in different countries. The following paragraphs represent some of the major changes to the basic financial decisions:

I. ***Foreign capital budgeting*** requires the use of foreign cash flows and local tax rates, but U.S. inflation rates and U.S. dollars at the current exchange rates can be used. The required return or cost of capital then need only be adjusted, as with any investment, for the greater or lesser risk of the project in which the investment is made, which includes the greater or lesser risk of the country in which the investment is being made.

II. ***Foreign capital markets*** are a source for both debt and equity funds, for both foreign subsidiary operations and the general needs of the overall business. Foreign subsidiary capital structures often utilize more local debt when legally and practically available in order to reduce the risk of blockages of earned funds from repatriation to the parent company in another country. In addition, local-currency debt reduces the risk for the parent company if the exchange rates for the local currency change adversely.

III. ***Foreign-exchange rates*** can change dramatically and therefore pose a significant risk for the value of assets held in or future payments from foreign countries. These exposures may be in dealings with third parties or within a company's own foreign subsidiaries. Forward currency contracts or currency options, instruments used to purchase one currency for another currency in the future at guaranteed exchange rates, can be used to protect against such risk.

International Finance—Prominent Institutes

There are various global bodies regulating different aspects of international finance. These include:

- **IFC** : International Finance Corporation is a prominent entity supporting sustainable investments in the private sector of developing countries to stimulate their growth. It is the biggest source of multilateral loans and equity financing for projects undertaken by the private sector in developing countries. IFC plays a key role in providing technical assistance to businesses and governments of developing countries.
- **IMF** : International Monetary Fund monitors the balance of payments of its member countries. It is regarded as the lender of last resort for countries

facing a financial crisis, such as deficits and currency crisis. The relief amount is relative to the size of the country's contribution in the global trading system.

- **World Ban'k :** It funds the development of projects, mainly in developing countries, that are not financed by the private sector.
- **WTO :** World Trade Organization resolves multilateral and bilateral trade disputes in addition to the negotiation of different trade agreements among its various member nations.

International Finance-Benefits

Some of the benefits of international finance are:

- Access to capital markets across the world enables a country to borrow during tough times and lend during good times.
- It promotes domestic investment and growth through capital import.
- Worldwide cash flows can exert a corrective force against bad government policies.
- It prevents excessive domestic regulation through global financial institutions.
- International finance leads to healthy competition and, hence, a more effective banking system.
- It provides information on the vital areas of investments and leads to effective capital allocation.

International finance promotes the integration of economies, facilitating the easy flow of capital. The free transfer of funds would eventually result in more equality among countries that are a part of the global financial system

Finance in India

India Finance or finance in India has become a key driver of economic growth. The economy of India is the fourth largest in the world in terms of GDP. India adopted protectionism and self-reliance philosophies for strengthening and growing its economy following its independence in 1947. The country opened its doors in 1991, allowing free trade on the current account. Although the agriculture and allied sectors employ roughly 60% of the total Indian workforce, they account for merely 17% of the nation's GDP (as of 2007). The service and industrial sectors account for 54% and 29% of the GDP, respectively.

With the turn of the millennium, a new era began in the growth of the Indian economy. From fiscal 2003-2004 to fiscal 2007-2008, India recorded high single-digit GDP growth rates. Although India's GDP growth slowed in 2008 due to global recession, it remained in the high single-digit range.

India Finance : Currency

The official currency of India is the INR (Indian National Rupee). The currency is issued by the country's central bank, the Reserve Bank of India (RBI), which regulates foreign exchange in the country. Although there are no currency conversion limitations for the Indian rupee, the RBI has placed restrictions on the capital account. Although local firms can take capital out of the country to expand in the international markets, local households cannot diversify their portfolio globally. From 1950-1951 to the mid-1970s, the INR was linked to the Pound Sterling. From 1975 to 1982, the effective rate of the INR was linked to a "basket of currencies" of India's key trading partners. From 1982, the rupee was linked to the US dollar. In 1991, the RBI began removing restrictions and the valuation of the currency became determined by a 'managed' or 'dirty float' regime.

India Finance : Stock Market

The Indian stock market comprises of two major stock exchanges, the Bombay Stock Exchange (BSE) and the

National Stock Exchange (NSE), of which the former is more popular. Stock market trading and the functioning of the stock exchanges, brokers, investment advisors and portfolio managers are regulated by the Securities and Exchange Board of India (SEBI). India is *second* only to the US in terms of the number of companies listed on its stock exchanges. India has become a preferred location for global investment firms after it liberalized its financial policies in the early 1990s.

India Finance : Commodity Market

Trading in the Indian commodity market did not gain momentum till the early 1990s due to several restrictions imposed by the government. The Indian government has taken several measures, including the setting up of 21 regional and four national commodity exchanges, to enhance the efficiency of the commodity trading market. One of the top online commodity exchanges is National Commodity and Derivatives Exchange Limited (NCDEX). Future tradings in the commodity market are regulated by the Forward Markets Commission.

Financial Crisis—Credit Crisis and Credit Crunch

A financial crisis is a sudden wide-scale drop in the value of financial assets, or in the financial institutions managing those assets (and often in both). A financial crisis may be triggered by a variety of factors, but the situation is typically aggravated by negative investor sentiment—fear or panic. A financial crisis often sparks a vicious circle where an initial decline sparks fears by investors that other investors will pull their money out, leading to redemptions and increasing declines. The global credit crunch of 2008 is an example of a financial crisis.

Types of Financial Crisis

A financial crisis can usually be categorized as one of the five types:

- **Banking crisis :** This is triggered by a sudden withdrawal of bank deposits by several clients, a situation known as a bank run. Banks may not have sufficient funds to simultaneously pay back numerous depositors, since they loan their funds. This credit crunch situation impacts the economy, as it affects production as well as consumption.
- **Bursting of a bubble :** Financial bubbles are caused by tho overvaluation of assets, with prices exceeding the current value of the future income expected to be generated by these assets. Bubbles are doomed to eventually burst, with crashing prices. The Wall Street Crash of 1929 is an example of this type of financial crisis.
- **Currency crisis :** A country that maintains a fixed exchange rate may have to suddenly devalue its currency. This often leads to a sudden drop in foreign investments. The Asian currency crisis of 1997-1998 began with Thailand devaluing the baht and developed into most of Southeast Asia and Japan witnessing falling currencies.
- **Sovereign default :** A government may fail to repay its sovereign debt. This often leads to a sudden decline in capital inflows and a spike in capital outflows.
- **Wider economic crisis :** An economy may go through a period of slow or negative GDP growth. While slow economic growth may be called economic stagnation, negative GDP growth for more than a couple of quarters is recession.

Global Meltdown and its Impact on the Indian Economy

The basic cause of the crisis was largely an unregulated environment, mortgage lending to subprime borrowers. Since the borrowers did not have adequate repaying capacity and also because subprime borrowing had to pay two-to-three percentage points higher rate of interest and they have a history of default, the situation became worse. But once the housing market collapsed, the lender institutions saw their balance-sheets go into red. Although at one time it was thought that this crisis would not affect the Indian economy, later it was found that the Foreign Direct Investment (FDI) started drying up and this affected investment in the Indian economy. It was, therefore, felt that the Indian economy will grow at about seven per cent in 2008-09 and at six per cent in 2009-10. The lesson of this experience is that India must exercise caution while liberalising its financial sector. A redeeming feature of the current crisis is that its magnitude is much lesser than that of the Great Depression of the 1930s when unemployment rate in the United States exceeded 25 per cent. Currently, it stands at 6.5 per cent and is predicted to remain around eight per cent in 2009.

I. Impact on Indian Economy

The industries most affected by weakening demand were airlines, hotels, real estate. Besides this, Indian exports suffered a setback and there was a setback in the production of export-oriented sectors. The government advised the sectors of weakening demand to reduce prices. It provided some relief by cutting down excise duties, but such simplistic solutions were doomed to failure. Weakening demand led to producers cutting production. To reduce the impact of the crisis, firms reduced their workforce, to reduce costs. This led to increase in unemployment but the total impact on the economy was not very large. Industrial production and manufacturing output declined to five per cent in the last quarter of 2008-09. Consequently, a vicious cycle of weak demand and falling output developed in the Indian economy.

A weakening of demand in the US affected our IT and Business Process Outsourcing (BPO) sector and the loss of opportunities for young persons seeking employment at lucrative salaries abroad. India's famous IT sector, which earned about $ 50 billion as annual revenue, is expected to fall by 50 per cent of its total revenues. This would reduce the cushion to set off the deficit in balance of trade and thus enlarge our balance of payments deficit. If has now been estimated that sluggish demand for exports would result in a loss of 10 million jobs in the export sector alone.

To lift the economy out of the recession the Government announced a package of Rs. 35,000 crores in the first instance on December 7, 2008. The main areas to benefit were the following:

(*a*) Housing : A refinance facility of Rs. 4000 crores was provided to the National Housing Bank. Following this, public sector banks announced to provide small home loans seekers loans at reduced rates to step up demand in retail housing sector.

(*i*) Loans up to Rs. 5 lakhs: Maximum interest rate fixed at 8.5 per cent.

(*ii*) Loans from Rs. 5-20 lakhs: Maximum interest rate at 9.25 per cent.

(*iii*) No processing charges to be levied on borrowers.

(*iv*) No penalty to be charged in case of pre-payment.

(*v*) Free life insurance cover for the entire outstanding amount.

This means a borrower can get a loan up to 90 per cent of the value of the house. The government hopes to disburse Rs. 15,000 to 20,000 crores under the new package.

(*b*) Textiles : Due to declining orders from the world's largest market the United States, the textile sector have been seriously affected. An allocation of Rs 1400 crores has been made to clear the entire backlog in the Technology Upgradation Fund (TUF) scheme.

(*c*) Infrastructure : The government has been proclaiming that infrastructure is the engine of growth. To boost the infrastructure, the India Infrastructure Finance

Company Ltd. (IIFCL) has been authorised to raise Rs. 14,000 crores through tax-free bonds. These funds will be used to finance infrastructure, more especially highways and ports. It may be mentioned that 'refinance' refers to the replacement of an existing debt obligation with a debt obligation bearing better terms, meaning thereby at lower rates or a changed repayment schedule.

(*d*) Exports : Exports which accounted for 22 per cent of the GDP are expected to fall by 12 per cent. The government's fiscal package provides an interest rate subsidy of two per cent on exports for the labour-intensive sectors such as textiles, handicrafts, leather, gems and jewellery, but the Federation of Indian Export Organization (FIEO) felt the measures are not enough as they will not make the exports price-competitive and, therefore, will not boost exports. G.K. Pillai, the Commerce Secretary, has estimated a loss of 1.5 million jobs in the export sector alone during 2008-09 on account of the $15 billion decline in the expected exports.

(*e*) Small and Medium Enterprises (SMEs) : The government has announced a guarantee cover of 50 per cent for loans between Rs. 50 lakhs to Rs. 1 crore for SMEs. The lockin period for loans covered under the existing schemes will be reduced from 24 months to 18 months to encourage banks to cover more loans under the scheme. Besides, the government will instruct state-owned companies to ensure prompt payment of bills of SMEs so that they do not suffer on account of delay in the payment of their bills. In short, the fiscal package is aimed at boosting growth in exports, real estate, auto, textiles and small and medium enterprises. The aim is to encourage growth and boost employment which have been threatened by the recession in the world economy, more especially in the United States.

Just within a month, the *government announced another package* to bail out the Indian economy. The purpose of the new package announced on January 1, 2009 was to minimise the pain. With this end in view, the new package included the following measures:

1. To boost investment and spending to revive growth, the RBI cut the repo rate, which it charges on short-term loans to banks from 6.5 per cent to 5.5 per cent and also reduced the Cash Reserve Ratio (CRR)—the share of deposits which has to be kept with the RBI from 5.5 per cent to five per cent.
2. To revive an export which has resulted in a contraction of industrial output, drawback benefits have been enhanced for some exporters. Export-Import Bank also gets Rs. 5000 crores as credit from the RBI.
3. To help the realty sector, realty companies have been allowed to borrow from overseas to develop "integrated townships".
4. To boost infrastructure, the India Infrastructure Finance Company Ltd. (IIFCL) has been allowed to raise Rs 30,000 crores from tax-free bonds. Besides, Non-Banking Finance Companies (NBFCs) need no government approval to borrow from overseas for infrastructure projects. This will sustain the growth momentum on infrastructure.
5. To make more funds available, ceiling on foreign institutional investments (FIIs) in corporate bonds has been increased to $ 15 billion from $ 6 billion. The purpose is to seek much bigger FII investment.
6. To stimulate the Commercial Vehicles (CVs) sector, depreciation benefit on commercial vehicles has been increased form 15 per cent to 50 per cent on purchases. Besides, the States will get one-time funding from the Centre to buy buses for urban transport. In addition, public sector banks would provide finance firms funds for commercial vehicles. It is hoped that Tata Motors and Ashok Leyland's sales would revive.

II. Assessment of the Impact of the Fiscal Package

There is no doubt that the government is motivated with good intentions and is thus aiming to spend a huge amount of Rs. 1,00,000 crores for developing infrastructure in roads, ports etc. which pose a serious handicap to growth. Besides, the aim of other measures is to boost exports and help sectors like textiles and small and medium industries which are labour-intensive and generate more employment. But the success of the fiscal package will depend on the quality and speed of implementation so that delays in implementation may not aggravate the economic recession to move into the dangerous zone of depression.

One of the major stumbling blocks which may neutralise the positive effects of large expenditure on infrastructure is corruption. In case corruption is not simultaneously curbed to reasonably low levels, it may delay and reduce the much-desired effect in enlarging infrastructure. It may result in the Indian infrastructure network being geared into a temporary employment generation programme with much smaller impact on the economy as against the intended objectives.

For reducing corruption, two things need to be ensured—transparency and avoidance of arbitrariness. By cutting arbitrariness in decision-making, corruption can be curbed to a great extent. Transparency instills confidence in the government.

Secondly, there is a need to orient the fiscal package towards inclusive growth so that the weaker sections benefit. This would require special emphasis, for instance, on rural infrastructure—rural roads and housing, instead of only highways and urban housing. Similarly, a much larger expenditure on primary and secondary education, health and sanitation can also result in a more inclusive growth process.

Thirdly, the chances of our exports increasing are very limited unless the G-3 economies, namely, the US, EU and

Japan, are able to bring about a positive shift in their growth in the near future for which the predictions at present are not very optimistic. The World Bank has projected the world output to grow at 0.9 per cent in 2009 as against 2.5 per cent in 2008. If these predictions come out to be true, there is a fear of the recession in 2008 turning into a depression in 2009. But the Indian economy is predicted to grow at about seven per cent in 2008 and about six per cent in 2009. Since the G-3 economies of the US, EU and Japan are affected seriously by the present recession, the chances of Indian exports increasing in these countries appear to be very dim. The natural conclusion is that the Indian economy should concentrate on developing the domestic market. Thus, inward looking policies should be preferred as against the outward looking approach of integrating the Indian economy to the world economy is followed during the last decade. It is heartening that the Prime Minister intends to insulate the Indian economy from the world economy.

Fourthly, although there is a demand for a much larger Fiscal Package to bail out the Indian economy, there are serious limitations faced by the government because it has to fight terrorism on the one hand and financial meltdown on the other. The government has to undertake a huge-expenditure at the Central as well as State levels to enhance security. It is difficult to precisely estimate this expenditure at this stage since it entails larger recruitment of police and paramilitary forces along with equipping them with the most uptodate weapons. But there is a massive increase in expenditure to combat terrorism, along with a fiscal package to boost the Indian economy; there is also likely to be shortfall in tax revenues. Consequently, the Budget deficit is bound to increase.

Conclusion

In sum of the view that given the ensuing serious repercussions of the global economic crisis on the economy and especially the poor who are the unorganised workers, a major response is urgently required. The core of this response in our view should be a major fiscal stimulus comprising of: (*i*) Programmes *to boost pro-poor public* investment in physical and social infrastructure, (*ii*) Programmes/schemes which *protect and promote incomes of the poor,* (*iii*) *Expansion in scope and coverage of social security* schemes for the unorganised workers so that they are immediately assured of a minimum level of social protection. These measures will not only protect the neediest, they will also provide the basis for reverting to a trajectory of high investment and high growth which has a decidedly pro-poor character.

India's recently liberalized FDI policy allows up to a 100% FDI stake in ventures. Industrial policy reforms have substantially reduced industrial licensing requirements, removed restrictions on expansion and facilitated easy access to foreign technology and foreign direct investment FDI. The government has been provided relief with the sharp fall, in the international price of crude oil and this should be taken advantage of in reducing expenditure to subsidise oil imports. The government amended the rules to allow 100 per cent FDI in the construction business. This automatic route has been permitted in townships, housing, built-up infrastructure and construction development projects including housing, commercial premises, hotels, resorts, hospitals, educational institutions, recreational facilities, and city and regional-level infrastructure. Additional employment generation by helping SMEs (Small and Medium Enterprises) will be a step towards inclusive growth since they are labour intensive.

REFERENCES

- Bodie, Zvi, Kane, Alex, and Marcus, Alan J. (1999). *Investments.* New York: Irwin-McGraw-Hill.
- Bruner, Robert F. and Eades, Kenneth M., Harris, Robert S., and Higgins, Robert C. (1998). "Best Practices" in Estimating

the Cost of Capital: Survey and Synthesis." *Journal of Financial Practice and Education* Spring.

- Kaushik, Surendra K., and Krackov, Lawrence M. (1989). *Multinational Financial Management.* New York: New York Institute of Finance.
- Sankaran, S. (1994). *Indian Economy: Problems, Policies and Development,* Margham Publications.

WEBSITES

- www.indiainfoline.com
- www.scholargoogle.com
- www.ezinearticles.com
- www.wikipedia.com

SECTION–IV
INFORMATION TECHNOLOGY

CHAPTER

14

Challenges to Introduction of Enterprise Resource Planning in Academic Institution

Prof. Basant Mehta
Mr. Pawan Shanker Sharma

ABSTRACT

Technology has penetrated almost each and every walk of life today. To keep pace with the growing competition academics institution too have open the flood gates for technology solutions to manage processes in an efficient manner.

On the positive note the technology introduction had not only made execution of processes faster and also had provided centralized control to manage things. ERP had been traditionally associated with the process industry .Now it is making inroads to different sector. The Introduction of ERP in education system had helped to revamp the system and manage various activities in better manner.

Enterprise Resource Planning introduction in academic institution is not a cake walk. The technology introduction is being challenged by change issues. The people concerned feel insecurity on job front and position. The paper shall also explore the reasons behind this resistance and shall elaborate on ways as to how one can overcome the challenges and thus help in making of a vibrant organization that is spontaneous in response and can manage the system better.

Introduction

The widespread adoption of enterprise resource planning (ERP) system by large and medium-sized organizations, described as the "ERP revolution". The basic and foremost challenge was that a considerable number of information systems (IS) by one single ERP .The next major challenge is to see that a risible efficiency is increased in terms overall productivity. The sizeable increased is must otherwise there is no use of making a changeover .The traditional system was working fine. The change issues related to human behaviour are bound to affect the system.

The next issue that has to be catered is the provision for flexibility as to how the system is capable of effective monitoring and exploitation of the university's assets and revenue-expenditure flow, and improved decision-making. It is plausible that, ERP system implementations require a reformulation of business processes and organizational structures but most importantly a change of management style and culture. Furthermore, collaboration within the organization and between the organization and the ERP provider also appears as a critical success factor in ERP applications. In addition, the importance of top management support, including employee training/participation should not be underestimated.

ERP systems also offer the opportunity for organizations to re-engineer their activities and revamp their information systems and accounting practices. For the staff, clearly opportunities arise to acquire marketable skills related to the process of installing and using new technology. The ability of a university to teach and conduct research more effectively as an indirect result of installing these systems is also postulated. This suggests that the adoption of ERP systems may, to some degree, be conducive in attaining broad-reaching goals beyond the immediate impact zone of the system itself. Such issues relating to the nature of work and the attainment of strategic institutional goals are important in every institutional context, not just in universities.

This suggests that creating high expectations can result in achieving higher user satisfaction. But on hind side the failure to live up to expectation due to undue reasons may result in the failure on account of reasons unasked for. The point that has to be taken care is the relationship between pre-implementation expectations and their perceived benefits based on post-implementation experience. They found that unrealistically high expectations would result in lower levels of perceived benefit than those associated with realistic expectations.

Research Questions

The important question that may arise out of the research is that the extent to which the introduction of a new ERP system can assist a public organization, such as the university, in achieving its aims, while focusing attention on improved efficiency in the managerial, operational, and IT infrastructure field.

This study examines the following research questions:

- What are the perceived benefits to the accounting information and management of a large public organization that derive from the adoption of an ERP system?
- How are the perceived benefits grouped in relation to the various dimensions?
- Are there differences between users' expectations and perceptions, as regards the benefits to the accounting information and management that are associated with the adoption of a new ERP system?
- The challenges faced are many as everybody is bound to resist the status quotas things that may lead to the unsatisfaction is loss of job and position with the introduction of the new system. The perceived benefits could be minimized on account of loss of authority due to introduction of new integrated system.

Data

In order to provide accurate information, the case study used unstructured informal survey was carried out among IT users to measure individual disconfirmation values and technological limitation faced with the introduction of new technology.

Research Methodology

There is a strong case study tradition in the academic field of IS management. The case study methodology, which is an umbrella term, does not impose any specific research technique, but rather defines a context Case study is now accepted as a valid research strategy within the IS research community. Case research moves away from rigour towards practicality, which may suggest more relevance for practitioners. The natural setting gives case researchers the opportunity to conduct situational and in-depth studies of complex phenomena that are not always possible because of the restrictions on studies conducted under laboratory conditions. In natural settings, researchers are able to explain more clearly the causal links through real-life interventions, describe the real-life context in which an intervention occurred and explore those situations in which the intervention being evaluated has no clear, single set of outcomes.

The modules of the ERP system include the following three main categories:

1. *Accounting-financial :* Double entry accounting system, cost and management accounting, public-budget accounting.
2. *Procurements of the purchase office :* Purchase schedule, management of suppliers, offers and contracts.
3. *Management information system :* Active reports, OLAP - online analytical processing, hierarchical data views, query viewer, graph reports.

The new introduced system also caters library management and other issues related to academic management of the institution.

Results and Discussion

Researchers have often attributed many implementation problems to users' resistance to change. Issues related to user expectations thus need to be addressed, since the university has illustrated how instead of increased efficiency, there was initially a drop in productivity amongst university staff, as a result of time spent learning about the new system.

Conclusions and Implications

The research that was conducted, aimed at locating the dimensions that had an effect on the accounting process and management of the university following the introduction of the new ERP system. The latter was deemed necessary along with the simultaneous application of the double.

Future research could focus on other dimensions of ERP system benefits such as the organizational and strategic field. A future study with financial data could compare the efficiency ratios before and after the ERP system's operation at the university in order to evaluate the calculated benefits from its implementation. Future research may further examine expected as opposed to actual benefits derived from ERP applications (on an individual basis), as well as the impact of technical, organizational and financial problems in fully exploiting ERP systems within an accounting context.

- Perceived risk associated with decision to adopt the change; and
- Habit, which refers to current practices that one is routinely using.

Expectations and Perceptions of IT users

Information technology (IT) user expectations are potentially an important factor affecting the perceived benefits arising from the use of new information systems (IS). Therefore; it is no surprise that managing user expectations has become a difficult but essential task. Managers who develop effective strategies along these lines can potentially enhance the success from the implementation of new ARE.

Conclusion

This empirical study focussed on IT users among the university staff, since the benefits from ERP adoption are directly linked to that user group. The acquisition of new skills, greater job satisfaction and empowerment were presented as the benefits from ERP adoption. It was suggested that by participating in the ERP project or working in areas that make use of new administrative systems, staff would acquire new skills for enhancing employment or promotion prospects, as well as job security. It was also suggested that staff empowerment would also be a consequence of the need for more varied and responsible roles required in the implementation of revised business processes.

REFERENCES

- Waldner, Jean-Baptiste (1992). *Principles of Computer Integrated Manufacturing.* Chichester : John Wiley & Sons Ltd. ISBN 047193450X.
- Waldner, Jean-Baptiste (1990). Les nouvelles perspectives de la production. Paris : DUNOD BORDAS. ISBN 9782040198206.
- Lequeux, Jean-Louis (2008). Manager avec les ERP, Architecture Orientee Services (SOA). Paris: EDITIONS D'ORGANISATION. ISBN 978-2-212-54094-9. CIO Magazine's ABCs of ERP.
- Clemons, E.K.; Kimborough (1986). "IS for Sustainable Competitive Advantage". *Information and Management* **11** (3): 131-136. doi:10.1016/0378-7206(86)90010-8

CHAPTER

15

Business Intelligence as a Tool for Top Level Management to Stay Competitive

Prof. Basant Mehta
Prof. S.S. Sarangdevot
Mr. Pawan Shanker Sharma
Dr. Tarun Shrimali

ABSTRACT

In this paper, we provide an overview of the important recent developments and the major future trends in academic research and software market for business intelligence (BI) technologies.

Introduction

Business Intelligence technologies provide historical, current, and predictive views of business operations. Common functions of Business Intelligence technologies are reporting, OLAP, analytics, data mining, business performance management, benchmarking, text mining, and predictive analytics. Business Intelligence often aims to support better business decision-making. Thus a BI system can be called a decision support system (DSS). The term business intelligence is often used as a synonym for competitive intelligence.

According to empirical studies, the BI usage within the utility industry is low. Organizations that develop the infrastructure and culture to support competing on analytics and fact based decision-making are more likely to survive the economic crisis and be poised for growth when the economy turns around. The top level management through the BI can manage the business in better manner and stay competitive.

BI has emerged as a way to meet users' demands while mitigating risk, and one that the economic downturn may accelerate, is the use of managed, hosted and outsourced services, including outsourcing analytics, along with data integration, reporting and data modelling. Programmable decisions can always be affected by both objective and subjective factors. Failure to recognize this fact may have contributed to the devaluation of "operations research" efforts and could spell the same fate for BI, if the field is not careful.

The pressure to improve business process and resource allocation, and the need to make better decisions have moved BI from mainstream to mission critical, which explains why growth is expected to be double that of the software market overall. BI systems are becoming increasingly more critical to the daily operation of organizations. We close the paper claiming that the need for a new generation of BI tools is strongly felt but many research issues must be further explored before creating a comprehensive solution.

Ultimate decision maker are the people sitting on the post of top level.If the timely information is provided to the top level managers the strategic, operational and tactical decision can be taken on time. The timely entry to the market always helps to define the laws of market. The precise and specific information can help the top level management to manage the market and to create a monopolistic scenario for itself.

This paper not only discusses the recent developments in the BI research and BI industry to keep us apprised of what are happening, but also provides the future trends in the BI research and BI industry to keep us informed of what are coming, thus to help us better prepare for meeting new challenges of BI technologies in the near future.

The ideal BI solution should, in a single integrated application, support the diverse needs of your finance organization including planning, reporting, monitoring, modelling and analysis. It should provide a financially accurate core of information and the ability to expose it to all employees, from finance to sales to operations and beyond. Better business Intelligence model shall help the organization to attain effective timeliness, better management of resources and shall also help the organization to enhance the productivity using the ICT facilities.

Business Intelligence (BI) has developed over the last few decades from financial statements, operations reports, marketing analysis, and manufacturing reports, to a completely integrated data mining solution that brings together live data from all over the company. To stay competitive companies have to take a hold over the basic relation between customer and supplier. Business has grown many folds from the traditional Barter system to modern retail chain managed system.

Modern Business Intelligence gathers data from various data points in the company to create multifaceted contextual information for better decision-making. In order to do this, a company brings together many different technologies and disciplines to deliver more information than most people can comprehend.

Business Intelligence and Its Application

Business Intelligence implementations have two major aspects; *Strategic and Tactical/Operational.* To take a leap ahead from the competitors the proper product placing in the market has to be taken care of. Heads to be put together to promote the brand properly and this would require the timely available of information from the nook and corner of the organization. Strategy is the plan for how the company will move forward and how it will place itself in the market place. Tactics and Operations are the nuts and bolts of how a company implements strategy. Business Intelligence shall provide the top level management with the much needed information.

It will support your processes and best practices and empower employees to ignite the power of the entire organization with a single repository of financial truth, especially financial truth.

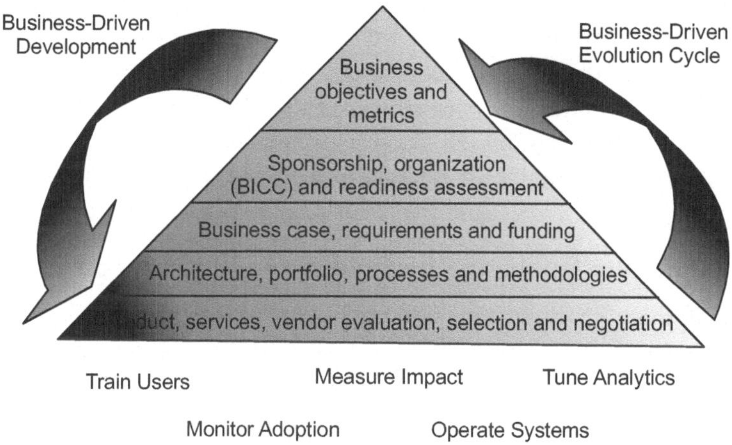

Diagram Provided by Gartner Group (Burton, Raynes, 2006)

The integration of the information at various level of the organization is must. Furtherance to the same it is must that the exchange of information should also be there. One has to look into the process and streamlined information flow shall help the organization to achieve edge over others and shall also Help the organization to be dynamic viable one and shall be ahead of others.

The Technology of BI

Business Intelligence gets its strength from being able to pull data from disparate sources store it for use in a loosely coupled way, and then pull it out in an accurate and meaningful way. An information warehouse can deliver strategic intelligence to the decision-makers and provide an insight into the overall situation. It is a broad category of applications and technologies for gathering, storing, analyzing and providing access to data to help the decision-makers in making decisions. Typically, BI applications include decision support systems, query and reporting.

The need to improve the decision-making capabilities using the ever increasing computing power, availability of RDBM Systems across heterogeneous platforms led to the use of more and more information in the decision-making process. Further, even if one does the analysis on large volume of data one should know the complete designing of the data model and the contents of it. It is practically not possible for any one to know the complete data modelling and the contents and ad hoc query analysis is simply not possible.

Deploying Business Intelligence in the Enterprise

It is this paradigm that will enormously increase the chances of success. The implementation should be done quickly with some immediately applicable data and tools. This will minimize the lethargy inherent in long projects, and give results that people can use immediately.

It is extremely important to have these critical elements in place when implementing a Business Intelligence programme into a company of any size. However, when it is done in a large setting, these elements are absolutely necessary to prevent a multi-million dollar disaster.

Conclusion and the Future of BI

Business Intelligence has come a long way since the 1960s. The democratization of computing and the greater affordability of powerful computing and storage has helped to cause BI to expand almost exponentially. From spreadsheets to complex reporting tools, the past growth of BI is indicative of an expanding future.

In today's world the only organization that can survive is that which is well informed can only survive and sustain the market pressure. The best found solution till date is BI. The seamless flow of information can provide us with means to take a leap ahead. The technology and the world is changing very fast. To be able to move together and take a cumulative decision the organization has to be knitted together in such a manner the organization connected in closed loop and is communicating all the time.The competitive world demands the organization should share the value and should extend the requisition if any in a timely manner and thus can moving.

REFERENCES

1. Baker, Stephen, "Math Will Rock Your World," Business Week, Jan 23, 2006.
2. Burton, Betsy, Rayner, Nigel, "Key Steps to Making Business Intelligence Strategic," Gartner Group, May 1, 2006.
3. Collins, Jim, Good to Great, Harper Collins Publishers, Inc, 2001.
4. Dresner, Howard, "A Short History of Business Intelligence and Where It's Headed," extracted 5/15/07.
5. Haag, Stephen, Cummins, Maeve, Phillips, Amy, Management Information Systems for the Information Age, Sixth Edition, McGraw-Hill/Irwin, 2007.
6. Lewis, Michael, Moneyball, W.W. Norton & Co., 2003.
7. Levinson, Meredith "The Brain Behind the Big, Bad Burger and Other Tales of Business Intelligence," CIO.com, May 15, 2007, http://www.cio.com/article/print/109454.
8. Computerworld, "BI: Proven Tools for Competitive Advantage in Uncertain Times," MarketVibe.

CHAPTER

16

Viability of Information Communication Technology (ICT) in NREGA

Prof. Basant Mehta
Mr. Pawan Shanker Sharma

ABSTRACT

The paper aims at what are effects of Information Communication Technology (ICT) on the National Rural Employment Guarantee Act (NREGA) The scheme aims at enhancing the live hood security of people in rural areas by guaranteeing hundred days of wage-employment in a financial year to a rural household who's volunteer to do unskilled manual work.

Information communication Technology had found it's in roads to almost every walk of life. We can see that it had provided us with a tool to manage things at geographical distinct places. As per records available at the Official website the total number of people who had been given jobs directly under the scheme is 3.92 core across the country. So as to keep eye on the system functionally centrally it is essential that the total project is handled and managed by computer based system. On the hind side India being a mass oriented economy and major section of the population is either illiterate and uneducated. So, as to provide jobs to large section of population the use of information communication technology to a large extend can be curse as it would hit at the head count that may get the bread and butter out of the scheme.

Thus the need of hour is the seamless integration of the technology and segregation of work as per knowledge quotient so as to make this scheme successfully viable one. On the other hand the fair penetration of technology has to be insured keeping in mind the realities of rural India. The paper concludes with the fair observation on the balanced use of Technology.

Introduction

The Scheme is aimed at enhancement of livelihood security of the households in rural areas of the country by providing at least one hundred days of guaranteed wage employment in every financial year to every household whose adult members volunteer to do manual work and for matters connected therewith or incidental thereto. According to the Gazette of India by Act of Parliament received the assent of the President on 5th September 2005 and published for general information. NAREGA ensures job guarantee to the rural folks and thus had created opportunity for self sustained life free from the clutches of landlords and brokers.

The negative aspect is that masses finding the job under the scheme have no idea about computer nor is the mission to get them acquainted to the computer but the chances of befooling them have high percentage. The second factor that has been a cause of divide is the knowledge level and aspiration level among the people engaged under this scheme. On one side we have a person that is total illiterate and on other hand we have a computer savvy professional. The gap is going to stay for ever and thus the divide had lead to '*Master Slave*' sort of scenario.

Present Scenario

Metros had come out to be the frontrunner to bore the torch of ICT development. Now the scheme demands extension of the technology to nook and corner of the country. Today's youth's modern metropolitan mindset does not forsee life and future in the village. Though it had created job opportunity for ICT professional but had not been at par with the level of satisfaction. Many undue cases can be quoted to support the fact that the scheme had paved the path for frauds. Though the guidelines mentioned under the scheme clearly sets demarcation as to how the things should be managed.

There had been numerous number of examples that can be quoted from the newspaper which highlighted the fact that the poor and downtrodden are being cheated. So, it is not the technology but the man that has to be made master. One should see to it as to how there could be a proper accommodation of technology in the system.

Analysis

The first and the foremost thing is to understand the life cycle of the system and also to be highlighted is the fact that the Gap between "As-Is" and to be "To-Be' system. We have also seen that the scheme is based for rural upliftment and unnecessary increase in the project cost can deviate the project from the core mission.

Modern society cannot deny how the introduction of ICT have changed their life. The world has now became a global village. The integration has of course made the work more easier. we can now sit in a room and monitor the things. If there are pros there shall always be cons also.

If one goes through the complaint section on the official NAREGA site one can see complains regarding the Manipulation in job cards and muster roll, on-display of proper board, Non-payment of wages through bank or post office, No facility of creche, drinking water, shade etc., Asking of money to open bank account under NREGA, Misuse of funds under NREGA, Misappropriation of funds by using fake muster rolls by sarpanch and Secretary, Use of J. B. C. machinery instead of labour, Construction of Grewal road without measurement and use of machinery instead of labour under NREGA and so on. One can see the problem existed for years in India. The technology had been able to forward the complain to the authorities but the net result is "Reply is awaited".

Though there are ample amount of opportunity but the system has to be corrected rather than made trikesh. There is lack of planning and implementation and control rather than the ICT usage failure or success, one thing that has to be kept in mind that the aptitude level of the people engaged under this scheme is not at par with the skill set required to manage ICT and thus the natural divide is not going to create any opportunity rather a threat of large monumental collapse. The use of ICT in Narega is not adding to the skill set of rural people nor should giving them the opportunity. One also see that the it is also a matter of concern that aftermath of scheme is that it had negatively affected the workmanship of local labourers and slowly it is making inroads in technical persons too. A right time has arrived to keep an eye on the whole system.

Infrastructure

The planning and project scheduling has to be done, the budgeting has to see where from and as to how long the funds shall be available. To reach far off placed the government owned telecom companies has come up with the technological solution to connect remote place.

The cost of development of the Infrastructure should also be taken under consideration under the overall project cost of the NAREGA. The basic aim of the scheme was to provide unskilled, physical work to the masses. The core mission has to be given the highest priority. There had been lot of lull and cry on the overall project management. There had been evidence of grave financial irregularities. One had not been able to check them with all available resources. It is now a high time that the proper project planning have to be formulated and brought to picture to give direction to mission. As we live in a democratic country. We have seen political parties taking undue advantage of schemes to boost their vote bank, vigilant efforts should be made to keep the politics out of fray.

Work Mechanism

Engineer and post graduate professionals are hired to work for MIS data entry work. With basic skill set people can easily manage the things. Nation that uses right person at right places progresses fast. We have to see to it where in the highly qualified person be used to best use their knowledge. We have also see the behaviour aspect of the professional engaged in the project. The system itself is too bulkier and spread of the system is also very vast. ICT can help to connect the things situated at far off places but a proper line has to be drawn to make the work mechanism realistic and reliable.

Creating the Right Paradigm

There are more and more talks of social audits and monitoring by eminent citizen. One cannot just sit in an AC room and let the things go by our hands. Things have to correct from roots and then managed by ICT. A balance has to drawn between the available technology solution and realities of the ground. Amenties have to be created for the ICT facilities and the technology introduction should be a phased manner. It is well known that we are not a capital centric economy so we should see to it that optimal use to technology can help in getting best results.

Conclusion

Proper planned effort is required to make this scheme a success. Optimal use of technology can help to develop a system that could successfully manage the things can help us in better management. One should always thrive to make technology a friend and not the master. It is also not recommended that the zero usage of the technology should take place but a judicious usage of technology should take place.

REFERENCES

1. Official website for Narega—http://nrega.nic.in/nctnrega/home.aspx.
2. National newspaper dailies.

Index